EXPRESSIVE
ONE-WORD

PICTURE
VOCABULARY
TEST

Third Edition

MANUAL

Rick Brownell, Editor

Academic Therapy Publications
Novato, California

Acknowledgments
We would like to express our sincere thanks to the many examiners, school systems, and students who participated in various phases of the revision of this test. The participants in this effort are too numerous to name here. A listing of many of the participants can be found in Appendix B.

Research and Statistics: Nancy Martin, PhD
Data Management and Statistics: Amy Brugger, MS
Data Entry Manager: Pam Nye
Production Manager: Jim Arena
Cover Design: Kurt West Design
Illustrations: Lineworks, Inc.

Academic Therapy Publications
20 Commercial Boulevard
Novato, CA 94949-6191
800 422-7249

International Standard Book Number: 1-57128-135-5

8 7 6 5
1 0 9

Contents

Overview

The *Expressive One-Word Picture Vocabulary Test* (EOWPVT) is an individually administered, norm-referenced test that provides an assessment of an individual's English speaking vocabulary. It is standardized for use with individuals ages 2 years 0 months through 18 years 11 months.

To administer the test, the examiner presents a series of illustrations that each depict an object, action, or concept. The examinee is asked to name each illustration. The test begins at a point at which the examinee is expected to meet with success in naming each illustration. The examiner then presents items that become progressively more difficult. When the examinee is unable to correctly name a number of consecutive illustrations, testing is discontinued. Total time for administration and scoring is typically 15 to 20 minutes. Raw scores can be converted to standard scores, percentile ranks, and age equivalents.

This edition of the EOWPVT includes national norms based on a representative sample of individuals residing in the United States. The test has also been conormed with the *Receptive One-Word Picture Vocabulary Test* (ROWPVT) so that meaningful comparisons can be easily made between an individual's expressive and receptive vocabulary. Other notable changes to this edition include the addition and replacement of many test items as well as new administration procedures that permit the examiner to prompt or cue examinees so that they will attend to the relevant aspects of each illustration. Additionally, all illustrations have been newly rendered in full color with drawings that are easy to interpret and that better hold the examinee's interest.

The components of the complete EOWPVT include the manual, a series of 170 test plates bound in a spiral booklet with a fold-out easel, and a package of record forms.

Expressive One-Word

Description

What's measured

This is a test of an individual's ability to name objects, actions, and concepts pictured in illustrations. The individual's performance, when compared to the norms group, gives an indication of the extent of his or her English speaking vocabulary.

Age range

This test was developed for use with English-speaking individuals ages 2 through 18.

Administration

Examinees are shown a series of illustrations and asked to name each as it is presented. Testing begins at a point where items are easy for an examinee to identify. As testing proceeds, items become progressively more difficult. When the examinee is unable to correctly name several consecutive items, testing is discontinued.

Norms

National norms are provided for interpretation of performance. Raw scores can be converted to standard scores, percentile ranks, and age equivalents. Difference scores for direct comparison to the *Receptive One-Word Picture Vocabulary Test* are also included.

Record Form
Clear directions are included on the form along with a listing of prompts to be used with items.

Picture Vocabulary Test

Manual
Includes detailed administration instructions, development procedures, and national norms.

Test Plates
Full-color illustrations are appealing and easy to recognize.

EXPRESSIVE ONE-WORD PICTURE VOCABULARY TEST

TEST PLATES

Academic Therapy Publications

What's New

Format

- New full-color illustrations have been rendered for all items.
- Lower and upper levels have been combined into a single edition for use with individuals ages 2 through 18.

Content

- Many new items have been added to increase the range and accuracy of assessment.
- Several of the previous items have been replaced.

Administration

- Instructions for using examiner prompts and cues are included and increase the accuracy of assessment.

Norms

- National norms based on a representative U.S. sample are provided.
- The test is conormed with the *Receptive One-Word Picture Vocabulary Test* for easy comparison of expressive and receptive vocabulary.

 # Preface

This is the third edition of the *Expressive One-Word Picture Vocabulary Test* (EOWPVT). The test was originally published in 1979 and revised in 1990. The first and second editions were developed for use with children ages 2-0 through 11-11. An upper extension of the test, for ages 11-0 through 15-11, was published in 1983. The current edition, published in the year 2000, combines the lower and upper levels and extends the use of the test through age 18-11.

Many changes have been made to the test to improve its effectiveness. These changes are in response to comments from users over the years and from professional reviews of the test, research studies, user surveys and discussion groups, and observation of administration of the test. A summary of these changes follows.

• Illustrations in the previous editions were in some cases difficult to recognize. In this edition, all illustrations have been rerendered in a uniform style that depicts all objects and scenes in a form easy to identify. With clearer illustrations, an examiner can be assured that it is the individual's vocabulary being assessed, not the individual's ability to infer or guess an object's identity. Furthermore, all illustrations have been rendered in full color. This has been done with subtle colors that add definition to the illustrations. This increases the appeal of the illustrations and helps maintain the individual's interest during test administration.

• In the previous edition, users of the test felt that examinees sometimes were confused by the intent of a particular item and would give an incorrect response when, in fact, the individual, with some direction, was indeed able to respond correctly. This edition includes new administration procedures intended to reduce item ambiguity and thereby increase the accuracy of assessment. This is accomplished by the use of prompts and cues, a procedure fully explained in the administration section of this manual.

• Norms in the previous edition were based on a regional sample, and users found that normative scores at some levels overestimated an individual's ability. The norms for this edition, in contrast, are based on a representative sample of school-age individuals in the United States. The sample consisted of 2,327 individuals and was stratified by age, geographic region, ethnicity, level of parent education, community size, and gender.

• The EOWPVT has often been used along with the *Receptive One-Word Picture Vocabulary Test* (ROWPVT) to provide a comparison of expressive and receptive vocabulary. In the previous edition, comparisons were limited by the fact that the norms of the two tests were based on different samples. For this edition, the EOWPVT and the ROWPVT have been conormed, meaning that each individual in the normative sample was administered both tests. This assures equivalency of the test norms. As a result, meaningful comparisons of expressive and receptive vocabulary are easily made. Each manual includes difference scores required for various levels of confidence as well as a table showing the frequency of occurrence of various discrepancy levels within the standardization group.

• Some items in the previous edition had become outdated (e.g., typewriter) or were otherwise problematic. These items were deleted and a number of new items were added, including several items at the beginning and end of the test. Items in the current edition have been subjected to rigorous review and item analysis. Input was received from hundreds of examiners across the country, and a panel of reviewers representing various ethnic groups and community types was consulted. Items that could contribute to test results that might be biased were deleted from the final form of the test.

As a result of these changes, users of this edition of the EOWPVT will find a test that not only meets a high standard of technical development but also one that is easy to use and that has great appeal to examinees.

Section 1:

Introduction

The *Expressive One-Word Picture Vocabulary Test* (EOWPVT) is an individually administered, norm-referenced test designed for use with individuals ages 2 years 0 months through 18 years 11 months. The test offers a quick and reliable measure of an individual's English speaking vocabulary, which is assessed by asking the individual to name objects, actions, and concepts pictured in illustrations.

An important feature of the EOWPVT is the equivalence of its norms to those of the *Receptive One-Word Picture Vocabulary Test.* Because of this equivalence, an individual's score on one test can be accurately compared to a score on the other test. If a significant difference between the scores is noted, the user of the tests can conclude, with confidence, that a true difference in expressive and receptive vocabulary exists.

Description of the Test

The components of the EOWPVT include this manual, a set of 170 full-color test plates ordered in respect to difficulty, and a package of record forms. The test plates are contained in a spiral booklet with a flip-out easel that is used when presenting the illustrations to the examinee.

The test can be administered in 10–15 minutes and scored in less than 5 minutes. Because the test plates are ordered in respect to difficulty, only those items within the individual's range of ability need to be administered. This is accomplished by establishing a basal of eight consecutive correct responses. From this point, testing is continued until a ceiling of six consecutive incorrect responses is obtained. Raw scores can be converted to standard scores, percentile ranks, and age equivalents.

Vocabulary Assessment

Vocabulary assessment has held a prominent place in psychoeducational testing for many years. The importance of this role is underscored by continued research into the effect that vocabulary has on an individual's academic success (e.g., Baker et al., 1998). Vocabulary tests are popular for two reasons: First, they provide information about a skill that has a significant bearing on an individual's success in a variety of endeavors. Second, they are generally quick and easy to administer while providing objective, valid, and reliable results. Vocabulary tests come in several variations, but all simply ask an individual to name, identify, or define a number of words.

Vocabulary is one of several fundamental elements that determines an individual's ability to understand what is heard or read (receptive language) and to communicate verbally or in writing (expressive language). Vocabulary is more than a mere association of words and definitions. Knowing the meaning of a word requires knowledge of a broader topic; it is topic knowledge that provides the context for assigning meaning to a word. For example, knowing the word "spatula" suggests that the person knows of its use and, therefore, has knowledge about cooking, food, and a whole set of related information. Vocabulary reflects what an individual knows about his or her world and, in turn, contributes to the effectiveness with which the individual is able to think about, or comprehend, that world and learn from experience. By monitoring vocabulary acquisition, we gain an understanding of the extent of a person's general knowledge.

Acquisition of vocabulary comes not only from direct experience but also indirectly via listening and reading. While a person may know what a "spatula" is by having used one, that person may also know what a space vehicle is by hearing or reading about it, without ever having experienced one directly. Indirect experience, particularly via reading, plays a prominent role in vocabulary acquisition (Stahl, 1999).

Given the nature of vocabulary, it comes as no surprise that tests of vocabulary are often included as subtests in assessments of cognitive ability, language, and academic achievement. The relationship to each of these areas is discussed below.

Vocabulary and Cognitive Ability

Terman, in 1916, identified vocabulary as one of the single best predictors of cognitive ability. Research over the years has confirmed that a strong relationship exists between vocabulary and cognitive ability, particularly verbal ability (Bornstein & Haynes, 1998).

Vocabulary is acquired through experience in the home, at school, and in the community. While some vocabulary is acquired through intentional instruction from caregivers and teachers and through self-study, it is likely that the majority of words we know are learned incidentally. Those who have the greatest facility for this type of learning are at an advantage in developing their vocabularies and general knowledge.

Of course, opportunity to learn also weighs heavily into this equation. As it turns out, there is a reciprocal relationship between the extent of an individual's vocabulary and the amount of exposure an individual has to new words—the largest source of acquired vocabulary appears to be reading material (Stahl, 1999), and those who have the most sophisticated reading skills tend to be the most prolific readers and consequently are the most successful in further developing their vocabularies (Stanovich, 1986).

While cognitive ability no doubt plays a role in vocabulary acquisition, opportunity to learn is clearly an important contributing factor. Results from vocabulary tests, such as the EOWPVT, therefore, do not offer a direct index of cognitive ability. A test of vocabulary reflects word knowledge, which may be affected by a variety of other factors. Inferences about an individual's cognitive ability based on the results of a vocabulary test should be substantiated through more comprehensive assessment.

Vocabulary and Language

Vocabulary is only one aspect of language, but individuals tend to learn the various components of language, such as phonology and syntax, simultaneously and in a generally prescribed order. Children express their first words around age one, and by age three their vocabularies have grown from just a few words to a few thousand words. By age six, children's speech is structurally similar to that of adults, but without the richness of an extensive vocabulary.

Because language is concerned with imparting meaning, and words are the vehicles of meaning, it follows that there is a relationship between vocabulary and other aspects of language. The majority of children acquire language readily and accurately without apparent difficulty. However, some language acquisition disorders are seen by school psychologists and speech-language professionals in about 5 percent of school-age children. Disorders related to vocabulary acquisition and speech production include language delay, aphasia, and expressive/receptive language disorders. Rapin (1996) provides a review of a wide range of language disorders.

Vocabulary tests, such as the EOWPVT, can be useful in determining the current level of an individual's vocabulary. This information, when combined with tests of other aspects of language, can help establish a comprehensive profile of an individual's language abilities.

Vocabulary and Academic Achievement

Formal education is primarily a language-based activity that is dependent on extracting information from what is heard and read. Those with the richest vocabularies are at an advantage in all language-related academic endeavors. The importance of this advantage is easy to see when we consider the increasing language demands facing students as they proceed through the school years. Vocabulary, as well as general knowledge, is cumulative, and the learning of new words and topics is built on previous understanding. Individuals with the most well-developed vocabularies are the best prepared to understand progressively more complex information.

The relationship between vocabulary and reading comprehension has long been acknowledged in educational research (Nagy, 1988). The extent of vocabulary is related to differences in reading comprehension ability at all ages (Stanovich, 1986) because word knowledge reflects topic knowledge, which, in turn, facilitates understanding of what is read. The importance of this relationship is reinforced when we look at longitudinal data indicating that poor readers in first grade remain poor readers throughout the grades unless remedial efforts are implemented (Juel, 1988). These students have relatively limited vocabularies and poor reading comprehension.

While assessment of vocabulary does not serve as a general index of reading comprehension or other areas of academic achievement, vocabulary is clearly an important component in the reading and learning process. Results from vocabulary assessment can provide important information that, when combined with other test results, can help identify an individual's profile of abilities related to academic achievement.

Expressive and Receptive Vocabulary

While tests of expressive vocabulary tap the ability to use words, tests of receptive vocabulary tap the ability to comprehend the meaning of words. The key difference between these two types of vocabulary tests is that expressive vocabulary tests add the further task requirement of gaining access to words and retrieving them from memory. For example, on the EOWPVT, the individual looks at an illustration and must provide the word that best describes the object, concept, or action shown. With easy items, individuals are facile in providing the correct word, but as items become more difficult, individuals reach a point where, in some cases, they say, "I know what that is, but I can't come up with the word." This is the common "tip-of-the-tongue" phenomenon that we all experience—we know what we are looking at or thinking of, but we can't access the word that names it.

Receptive vocabulary, in contrast, requires only recognition of the meaning of a word. Because of this, an individual's receptive vocabulary is generally larger than his or her expressive vocabulary. Vocabulary tests, such as the EOWPVT and the ROWPVT, however, account for this difference. When all else is equal, individuals should show similar performance on these two tests when comparison is made through an age-based performance index such as standard scores. Obtained differences in performance, when significant, can be diagnostically important.

Purpose and Uses

The EOWPVT provides a measure that reflects the extent of an individual's vocabulary that can be accessed and retrieved from memory and used to produce meaningful speech. It is a measure that depends on a number of component skills and that has implications regarding an individual's cognitive, language, and academic performance.

The EOWPVT has a number of specific uses. Listed below are frequent ways in which this test is used.

Assessing the Extent of Spoken Vocabulary. The EOWPVT requires the individual to name objects, actions, and concepts that range from familiar to obscure and in this way provides an assessment of how an individual's vocabulary compares to what is expected of individuals at a particular age level.

Assessing Cognitive Ability. Because vocabulary acquisition is related to the efficiency with which an individual learns, it can provide a peripheral view of cognitive ability. Because ability is multifaceted, results used in this way should be viewed with caution, and further assessment should always be conducted to support findings.

Diagnosing Reading Difficulties. The relationship between vocabulary and reading is clear: those with restricted vocabularies have difficulty comprehending on-level reading materials. Additionally, individuals with poor reading skills read less than their better-reading peers and therefore have diminished opportunity to build vocabulary.

Diagnosing Expressive Aphasia. Because the EOWPVT was conormed with the ROWPVT, a valid comparison of expressive and receptive vocabulary can be made. Because performance on the EOWPVT depends on the individual's ability to access and retrieve specific words, a task not required on the ROWPVT, differences in performance may be observed. This comparison should take into account the statistical significance of the difference as well as the frequency with which a difference of the observed magnitude was obtained in the standardization sample. Provisions for making these comparisons are included in this manual.

Screening Preschool and Kindergarten Children. Since the EOWPVT is a test that engages even young children, and because vocabulary is an important skill, the EOWPVT is often used as part of a screening program for children entering preschool or kindergarten. It provides insights into the child's abilities and helps to build rapport.

Evaluating an English Learner's Vocabulary. For students learning English as a second language, the EOWPVT can be used to evaluate the extent of the individual's English vocabulary. When using the test in this way, it is important to note that the norms are based on individuals whose primary language is English; therefore, results, particularly those indicating low performance, cannot be interpreted in the same way as similar results obtained by an individual whose primary language is English.

Monitoring Growth. Because the EOWPVT serves an age range that encompasses the school-age population, it can be used as a longitudinal measure to monitor growth during a school year or from year to year throughout a group or individual's entire school career.

Evaluating Program Effectiveness. As a research tool, the EOWPVT can be used to evaluate the effectiveness of various types of programs. For example, for programs designed specifically to increase vocabulary or to improve reading comprehension, the EOWPVT can serve as one measure that would be expected to be sensitive to the effectiveness of such programs.

Limitations

As a test of English speaking vocabulary, the EOWPVT samples only a limited number of skills from what we regard as the total constellation of skills that define an individual's ability. Results from the EOWPVT should be used in conjunction with other measures to more fully understand an individual's profile of abilities. Since performance on this test can be affected by a variety of factors, including hearing problems or visual deficits, poor performance on the test must be interpreted in light of other findings. Results of a vocabulary test such as the EOWPVT cannot confirm, for example, that an individual has a learning problem, but the results can prompt the user of the test to identify important questions about the individual and then to pursue answers through further, more specific evaluation.

The EOWPVT assesses spoken vocabulary and can provide important information about an individual's level of language functioning. While a comprehensive evaluation of language skills requires more than an examination of the individual's ability to verbally use single words, administration of the EOWPVT provides a practical, objective, and efficient step in this process.

Section 2:
Considerations

This section provides information about topics that are important to consider in the general use of the EOWPVT. Included in this discussion is information about examiner qualifications as well as information that pertains to the effective administration of the test.

Examiner Qualifications

The EOWPVT is most often used to inform speech/language pathologists, psychologists, counselors, learning specialists, physicians, occupational therapists, and other educational, psychological, and medical professionals. In addition to these professionals, the test may be administered by those who do not have specific training in assessment. These individuals, however, must be trained by and be under the supervision of a professional familiar with the principles of educational and psychological assessment and interpretation. Prior to administration of the test, the examiner should become thoroughly familiar with the administration and scoring procedures presented in this manual and should conduct several trial administrations.

Interpretation of the test results must be conducted by individuals who have formal training in psychometrics and who have full knowledge of the use of derived scores and the limitations of test results.

Examinees

The EOWPVT is appropriate for use with English-speaking individuals ages 2 years 0 months through 18 years 11 months. Norms are based on a representative sample of individuals residing in the United States whose primary language in the home and school is English. When the test is used with individuals who do not meet this description, interpretation of test results must be made with caution.

Order of Testing

If a receptive picture vocabulary test, such as the *Receptive One-Word Picture Vocabulary Test*, is going to be administered along with the EOWPVT, it is recommended that the EOWPVT be administered first since learning may take place in the administration of the receptive test that could affect expressive vocabulary performance.

Testing Time

The EOWPVT requires approximately 10 to 15 minutes to administer and less than 5 minutes to score. This is not a timed test, so the examinee should be allowed ample time to review the illustrations on the test plates and to respond to each item.

Although administration can normally be completed in a single session of 15 minutes or less, with very young children it may be appropriate to extend the testing to more than one session. This will allow the child to become more at ease with the examiner, the testing environment, and the testing procedure.

Testing in more than one session may also be necessary with examinees who show reluctance, resistance, or negative behavior. In this case the examiner should attempt to motivate the individual by offering encouragement and praise as the sample items are introduced. If sufficient motivation is not present or if the examinee is otherwise uncooperative, testing should be discontinued and resumed at a later date.

Testing Environment

Testing should be conducted in an environment that is free of visual and auditory distractions. In addition, the examinee should be calm and rested. When practical, it is recommended that testing be conducted in the early part of the day since this is a time when individuals are rested and are better able to attend to a task that requires concentration.

Preparation for Testing

Before administering the test, the examiner should record the examinee's date of birth and determine the individual's chronological age in years and months. The record form provides space for this calculation, and further instructions are given in the Administration and Scoring section of this manual. Chronological age is used to identify the first item at which to begin testing and for obtaining scores from the norms tables following administration. The examinee's grade level and the reason for being tested should also be documented in the space provided on the record form.

Seating

The examiner and examinee should be seated at a table or desk that is a comfortable height for the examinee. Seating should be arranged so that the record form is kept out of the clear view of the examinee. In some cases, the examiner will want to sit kitty-corner or across from the examinee. In this configuration it is easy to keep the record form out of view. Another arrangement is to sit next to the examinee and to place the record form to the far right for a right-handed examiner or to keep the record form in a notebook that is held in one hand at an angle that prevents the examinee from seeing it.

Preparing the Examinee

Prior to testing, engage the examinee in general conversation so that he or she will feel at ease. After the examinee has been given a chance to feel comfortable with the testing environment, the test should be explained. All verbal directions should be presented in simple terms, and questions regarding the testing procedure should be answered. When the examiner feels the examinee is comfortable and understands the testing procedure, testing can begin.

On some occasions with younger children, it is helpful to have a parent present to make the child feel secure. If the parent's presence is necessary, it is important to caution the parent not to become involved in the testing. The parent should not prompt the child and should not engage in conversation with the examiner during the administration of the test.

Examinee Behavior

The examiner will be able to observe the examinee's behavior during the administration of the test. Hyperactivity, distractibility, poor attention, or mannerisms suggesting lack of self-confidence, fear of failure, and so on, should be noted on the record form in the space provided. These observations should be taken into consideration when interpreting the results of the test. When it is apparent that such behaviors are preventing the individual from accurately demonstrating his or her ability, testing should be discontinued and resumed at a later date.

Section 3:

Administration & Scoring

This section provides a discussion of administration and scoring procedures that lead to the accurate use of the EOWPVT. Since this edition incorporates administration procedures different from those in previous editions, all users, including those who have used previous editions, should become thoroughly familiar with these instructions. A sample record form is included at the end of this section for your reference.

Administration Instructions

Before administering the test, carefully read the administration instructions presented below. These instructions are also summarized on the record form for your reference.

Determining Chronological Age

Chronological age must be determined prior to testing to identify the item number at which testing should begin. Chronological age is also used to identify the appropriate table to use in determining normative scores. To calculate chronological age, write the Date of Testing and the examinee's Date of Birth in the space provided on the record form. Subtract the Date of Birth from the Date of Testing, beginning with the day, to determine the chronological age. In some cases, when the Date of Testing day is less than the Date of Birth day, borrow 30 days from the Date of Testing month (all months are assumed to have 30 days). Or when the Date of Testing month is less than the Date of Birth month, borrow 12 months from the Date of Testing year. After performing this calculation, the subtracted year and month represent the examinee's chronological age. *Do not round months up when days exceed 15.* Consider the following examples.

In the example below, no borrowing is required. The examinee's chronological age is 8 years 7 months. Even though days exceeded 15, months were not rounded up.

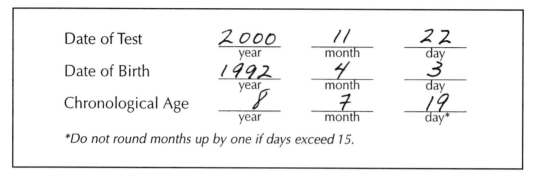

In the following example, borrowing is required since the Date of Testing month is less than the Date of Birth month. The Date of Birth is then subtracted and a Chronological Age of 9 years 6 months is obtained.

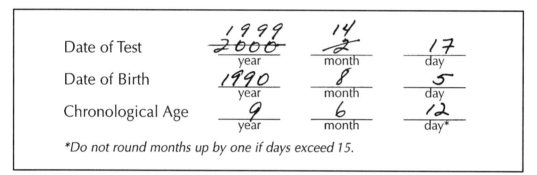

In the next example, both the Date of Testing month and day are less than the Date of Birth month and day. Thirty days are first borrowed from months, which reduces months to 4. Then, 12 months are borrowed from year, which reduces year to 1999. The Date of Birth is then subtracted and a Chronological Age of 10 years, 7 months is obtained.

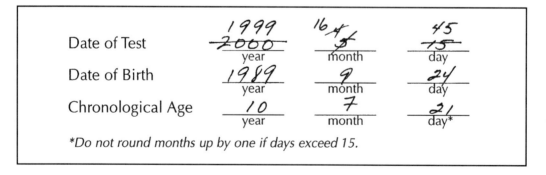

Critical Range Testing

Because the items on this test are arranged in order of difficulty, only a subset of consecutive items, or critical range, needs to be administered. The critical range varies for each individual. It begins with a series of items that are easy for the examinee and ends at a point where the examinee's responses are consistently incorrect. On the EOWPVT this range begins with a series of eight consecutive correct responses, referred to as the *basal*, and ends when a series of six consecutive incorrect responses has been obtained, referred to as the *ceiling*. Because items are ordered with respect to level of difficulty, when an individual makes several consecutive correct responses, it can be assumed that he or she would also respond correctly to the preceding items. These earlier items, therefore, need not be administered. Similarly, when an individual makes several incorrect responses, it can be assumed that the examinee would also miss subsequent items, which increase in difficulty.

In some cases a basal or a ceiling will not be established. This is common with examinees whose ability level falls at one extreme or the other. When no basal is established, item 1 should be considered the basal item. When no ceiling is established, the last item should be considered the ceiling item.

Establishing a Basal and Ceiling

To establish the basal level of eight consecutive correct responses, begin testing at the point indicated on the record form for the examinee's chronological age. Suggested starting points are also listed in Table 3.1. If you suspect that the examinee may have difficulty at this level of the test, you may want to start at a lower point. Also, for examinees who lack confidence, it is helpful to begin at a point where the individual can feel a sense of success before moving on to more difficult items.

TABLE 3.1
Suggested Starting Points

Age	Item Number	Age	Item Number
2-0–2-11	1	8-0–8-11	60
3-0–3-11	10	9-0–10-11	70
4-0–4-11	20	11-0–12-11	80
5-0–5-11	30	13-0–14-11	90
6-0–6-11	40	15-0–18-11	100
7-0–7-11	50		

If the examinee does not establish a basal of eight consecutive correct responses, return to the first item administered and work backward until the examinee does establish a basal or until item 1 has been administered. Then continue presenting the items in a forward direction, beginning with the item following the item that indicated the necessity for working backward.

Continue presenting the test plates in ascending order until the examinee makes six consecutive errors or the last item of the test is administered. The ceiling will be the last item of the six consecutive items or the last item on the test if a ceiling is not otherwise reached.

If the examinee establishes two or more ceilings as a result of having to work backward to establish a basal, the lowest ceiling is used in computing the raw score. Conversely, if the examinee establishes two or more basals, the one closest to the ceiling is used in computing the raw score. (See the sample record form at the end of this section for an example of the administration and scoring process.)

Examinee Instructions and Examples

Administration begins with an explanation of the task to the examinee.

Say, **"I am going to show you some pictures, and I want you to tell me the word that names each picture or group of pictures."**

Four examples are then presented. The examinee does not need to get all of the example items correct in order to proceed with administration of the test. During presentation of the examples, the examiner should provide guidance as needed to ensure that the examinee understands the task. Testing then begins at the suggested starting point and continues as described below.

Presentation of Test Items

The rate of speed in showing each test plate should be adjusted to the pace of each individual. Do not, however, allow an inordinate amount of time for the individual to respond since this may cause the individual to lose focus and ultimately become frustrated. Set a comfortable pace that keeps the examinee on task. To control the pace of presentation, the examiner, not the examinee, should turn the test plates.

During testing the examiner should offer encouragement and praise, but any kind of coaching should, of course, be avoided. Some examinees are easily distracted and will require greater motivational efforts on the part of the examiner to maintain attention. Excessive praise, however, when not realistic becomes meaningless. Every effort should be made to avoid praising the examinee for a correct answer and giving no response for a wrong answer. If the examinee shows concern about his or her performance, explain that no one gets all the answers correct. If the examinee asks for confirmation about the correctness of a response, indicate that the response was a good answer and move on to the next item. Do not tell the examinee what the correct answer is to any item at any time during or after testing.

When and if the examinee first says that he or she doesn't know the answer, encourage him or her to respond. If this happens more than two times, then simply mark the item incorrect, noting that the examinee doesn't know, and move on to the next item.

Using Prompts and Cues

Two types of verbal instructions can be used with each test item: prompts and cues. A *prompt* is used before the examinee has given a verbal response to the item. A *cue* is used after the examinee's first response when that response indicates that he or she is not attending to the correct features of the illustration. The use of prompts and cues is a simple process that increases the efficiency of administration and the accuracy of the test results. A thorough understanding of the use of prompts and cues is necessary to obtain valid results. The discussion that follows describes the use of prompts and cues. A summary is presented in Table 3.3 at the end of this section. Additionally, Appendix A presents a listing of examples of incorrect responses as well as examples of responses that should be cued by the examiner.

Prompts

A prompt indicates to the examinee whether he or she is to identify an object, action, or concept. A prompt should be used with each test item in order to keep the examinee on task and to maintain a steady pace. For the majority of items, the prompt *"What's this?"* is appropriate. Some items require a different prompt, which is listed with the item on the record form. Table 3.2 shows a listing of the three types of prompts to be used along with examples of corresponding items.

TABLE 3.2
Prompts Used in Administering the EOWPVT

Item Type	Prompt	Item Example
OBJECT	*"What's this?"* *"What are these?"*	dog pyramid(s)
ACTION	*"What's he/she doing?"*	paint(er/ing)
CONCEPT	*"What word names all of these?"*	fruit

Prompts are intended to focus the individual's attention and to speed up the testing process. Their use is particularly effective with younger examinees who have relatively short attention spans and who may not readily recognize the intent of the different types of items.

Do not use prompts with wording other than that provided in these instructions since that might affect item difficulty and yield results inconsistent with the standardization of the test. For example, for the item that shows a grouping of pens and pencils, the correct response is "write(ing)" or "draw(ing)." Use of a cue such as "These things are all used for—" should not be used since it provides verbal information that aids retrieval of the correct word. This lowers the item difficulty and results in an individual correctly naming the concept when he or she would be unable to do so when the correct prompt is used.

Cues

Sometimes examinees give an answer that indicates they are attending to a different aspect of an item than is intended. For example, for the item "toe" an illustration is presented that shows a foot with an arrow pointing to a toe. When the examinee responds "foot," a cue is used to clarify the intent of the item. The examiner offers the cue by pointing to the part that the arrow is pointing to and saying "What's this?" A cue makes the intent of the item clear, and the examinee is given a second opportunity to name the illustration. *Cues are given only when the examinee's first answer indicates that he or she is not focusing on the correct intent of the item; other incorrect answers are scored as incorrect, and no cue is offered.*

You must know when and how to offer appropriate cues to ensure that valid results are obtained. Only one cue per item can be used. If the examinee does not give the correct response after one cue has been given, count that response incorrect and move to the next item.

Object Cue

Wrong level in a hierarchy. Many objects can be identified with various levels of specificity because they fit into a hierarchy. When the individual gives a response that is too general, this cue should be given—

Say, *"What kind?"*

Example: **Item A, Dog**
Individual: Animal
Examiner: What kind?
Individual: Dog

When the individual gives a response that is too specific, this cue should be given—

Say, *"What else is this called?"*

Example: **Item A, Dog**
Individual: Cocker (type) or Rover (name)

Examiner: What else is this called?
Individual: Dog

Action given for an object. When the individual names the action of the object rather than the object, use this cue—

Point to the illustration and say, "What's this?"

Example: **Item 28, Kite**
Individual: Flying
Examiner: (points to illustration) What's this?
Individual: Kite

Whole or wrong part given when a part is identified. Some items show an arrow pointing to part of the illustration. If the individual says the name of the whole illustration or the wrong part—

Point to the part that the arrow is pointing to and say, "What's this?"

Example: Item B, Toe (Illustration shows foot with arrow pointing to toe.)
Individual: Foot (whole) or Heel (wrong part)
Examiner: (points to toe) What's this?
Individual: Toe

Action Cue

For some items the name of the action is required. Because most items require the naming of an object, the individual may name an object in the illustration instead of focusing on the action. In this case, say the following—

Say, "What's he (or she) doing?"

Example: **Item C, Eating**
Individual: Woman
Examiner: What's she doing?
Individual: Eating

Concept Cue

Some items show a collection of objects. A correct answer is the name of the concept that describes that collection. If the individual names one or more objects in the collection rather than identifying the concept, indicate that you want the name of the collection of objects with this cue—

Circle the illustration with your finger and say, "What word names all of these?"

Example: **Item D, Toys** (Illustration shows balls, blocks, truck, rocket, bear.)
Individual: Bear, Ball, . . .
Examiner: (Circles illustration with finger.) What word names all of these?
Individual: Toys

If the examinee continues to name the individual items after cued, do not offer another cue; mark the item incorrect and move on to the next item.

When Not to Cue

The majority of responses will not require cueing. For comparison, the list below shows the type of incorrect responses made to the example items shown above. Each of these responses is incorrect and would not be followed by a cue.

Example	Incorrect Response
Dog	Bear
Kite	Wind
Toe	Shoe
Eating	Cooking
Toys	Birthday

Acceptability of Responses

The record form lists all responses that can be accepted as correct. If after properly administering an item, the examinee's response is one other than what is listed as acceptable on the record form, it should be scored incorrect. Accepting responses other than those listed will affect the validity of the results. Appendix A shows a listing of the most frequently obtained incorrect responses.

Answer Presented in a Phrase or Sentence

Examinees should be encouraged to respond with a one-word answer. However, young children often have no concept of "word," and even older examinees sometimes respond with a sentence or phrase, particularly when items become difficult. For example, for the item "wrench" the examinee may say, "That's a wrench" or "That's a wrench for fixing things." As long as the target word is included in the phrase, it should be scored correct. Responses such as "That's a thing that my uncle has" or "That's for fixing things" are typical response forms used when an item is not known and should be scored incorrect.

TABLE 3.3
Use of Prompts and Cues Summary

Prompts. For each item, a prompt is given along with the presentation of the test plate. Prompts help examinees attend and they clarify the intent of the item. Usually the prompt "What's this?" is appropriate. When another prompt is to be used, the prompt is listed by the item number on the record form.

TYPE OF PROMPT	WHEN TO GIVE PROMPT	PROMPT
OBJECT PROMPT	When presenting the test plate	*Say, "What's this?"* *"What are these?"*
ACTION PROMPT	When presenting the test plate	*Say, "What's he/she doing?"*
CONCEPT PROMPT	When presenting the test plate	*Say, "What word names all of these?"*

Cues. The following cues are used, when called for, to identify the focus of the item. Cues are not given for a blatantly incorrect response.

TYPE OF PROMPT	WHEN TO GIVE PROMPT	PROMPT
OBJECT CUE	If the examinee gives a response that is too general	*Say, "What kind?"*
	If the examinee gives a response that is too specific	*Say, "What else is this called?"*
	If the examinee names the action of the object rather than the object	*Point to the illustration and say "What's this?"*
	If the examinee names a part within the illustration rather than giving the name of the whole object	*Circle the illustration with your finger and say, "What's this?"*
	When an arrow points to a part of the illustration and the examinee says the name of the whole object or the wrong part	*Point to the part that the arrow is pointing to and say, "What's this?"*
ACTION CUE	If the examinee names an object in the illustration instead of the action when naming the action is required	*Say, "What is he/she doing?"*
CONCEPT CUE	If the examinee names one or more objects in the collection rather than identifying the concept	*Circle the illustration with your finger and say, "What word names all of these?"*

Note: Object, action, and concept cues are to be given only when the examinee's response indicates that he or she is not attending to the appropriate features of the illustration. When a cue is required, the cue should be offered only once. If the examinee responds incorrectly following the cue, mark the item incorrect and move to the next item.

Spontaneous Self-Corrections

When an examinee says a word and then spontaneously offers a self-correction, score the item based on the self-correction even if the original response was correct and the self-correction is incorrect.

Inflectional Endings

Inflectional endings (e.g., -s, -es, -er, -ing) are optional, and the most common endings are listed in parentheses on the record form along with each word. For example, for the item "pyramid(s)," both "pyramid" and "pyramids" are correct answers. For the item "paint(er/ing)," "paint," "painter," or "painting" are correct answers. Word endings in addition to those listed on the record form may be given by examinees. As long as the root word is part of the examinee's answer, the response is counted correct; the use of inflectional endings has no bearing on the acceptability of the response.

Articulation

Misarticulation of words should not be cause for scoring an item incorrect for young children or for those individuals who exhibit consistent patterns of misarticulation when the mispronunciations are characteristic of the individual's speech pattern and the words are intelligible. For example, young children typically say "aminals" for "animals," and an examinee who substitutes /th/ for /s/ will say "inthect" instead of "insect." Examinees should not be penalized for this, but misarticulations should be noted.

For examinees whose speech does not show consistent misarticulations, responses should be counted wrong if the individual—

- Drops a syllable ("puter" for "computer")
- Substitutes a syllable ("momometer" for "thermometer")
- Adds a syllable ("antliers" for "antlers")
- Transposes a syllable ("boomranger" for "boomerang")
- Drops a sound ("tethescope" for "stethoscope")
- Substitutes a sound ("tunnel" for "funnel")
- Adds a sound ("scaddle" for "saddle)
- Transposes a sound ("detnist" for "dentist")

The general criterion is that a response is correct if the examinee demonstrates a facility to accurately name the object, action, or concept shown within his or her ability to produce the required speech sounds.

Recording Responses

For each item, space is provided for writing the examinee's response. The response should be recorded whether correct or incorrect; otherwise the examinee will be able to determine his or her success or failure on each item and may become distracted by the scoring process. Writing the response exactly as spoken by the examinee can also be useful for evaluation of the individual's articulation. While administering the test, the examiner should draw a slash through the item number for incorrect responses. This will provide a visual reference for identifying the basal and ceiling levels as the test is being administered. The examiner should also underline any responses that indicate a speech distortion or dysfunction and may want to use other coding systems (e.g., diacritical marks, phonological analysis symbols) for further analysis of responses that could be diagnostically significant.

Follow these guidelines when recording responses:

- **Correct first response.** In the space following the word, write down the response.

- **Correct cued response.** Place a slash after the first response to indicate that a cue was given. Then write down the next response. For example, for wrench, if the examinee says, "tool," you say, "What kind?" If the examinee then says, "wrench," you would record the response as "tool/wrench."

- **Incorrect first response.** In the space following the word, write the examinee's response or a dash if the examinee doesn't know. Put a slash through the item number. (Note: The first two times the examinee says he or she doesn't know, encourage the examinee to give his or her best answer. After that, accept "doesn't know" as an incorrect answer.)

- **Incorrect cued response.** Similar to above, place a slash after the examinee's first response and write the second response or a dash to indicate that the examinee didn't know (e.g., tool/screwdriver or tool/—). Put a slash through the item number.

1. Find the suggested starting point based on the examinee's age.

2. Say, **"I am going to show you some pictures, and I want you to tell me the word that names each picture or group of pictures."**

3. Have the examinee attempt examples A through D. Instruct the examinee as needed to understand the task.

4. Record all responses exactly as said by the examinee.

5. Mark errors with a slash through the item number.

6. Establish a basal of 8 consecutive correct responses.

7. Establish a ceiling of 6 consecutive errors.

Scoring

The examinee's raw score is the number of correct responses up to the last item in the ceiling. All responses below the basal are considered to be correct. As noted above, if the examinee establishes two or more ceilings, the lowest ceiling is used to compute the raw score. If the examinee establishes two or more basals, the one closest to the ceiling is used.

Space is provided on the record form for calculating the raw score as follows: From the last item, or the sixth item of the ceiling, subtract all of the errors including and below this item, except for errors that occurred below the basal. For example, if the sixth item of the ceiling is item number 70 and the examinee misses 20 items (including the six consecutive errors in the ceiling), his or her raw score would be 50.

Frequently Asked Questions

- **What if an examinee gives a response that seems acceptable but is not listed on the record form?** Only responses listed on the record form should be accepted as correct. Write any other response in the space provided and mark the item incorrect.

- **If I cue an examinee's response and the examinee seems to be getting close to the correct answer, should I give a second cue?** No, only one cue is to be given for an item. In field-testing it was found that it is most often unproductive to give more than one cue. Also, it is important that all examiners administer the test in the same way it was administered to the standardization sample.

- **What if a basal or a ceiling isn't obtained for an examinee?** This is OK. Young examinees often will not have a basal on a test because all of the easiest items, starting with item 1, have been administered. Likewise, older examinees sometimes reach the last item on the test without having a ceiling.

- **What if the examinee establishes a basal, misses a few, and establishes a second basal?** Sometimes two basals or two ceilings will appear in a protocol. Always use the lowest ceiling and the highest basal for determining the raw score.

EXPRESSIVE ONE-WORD PICTURE VOCABULARY TEST

RECORD FORM

Name: *Jane Smith* Gender: *f* Grade: *4*

School: *Braxton Elementary* Examiner: *Mrs. Deane*

Reason for Testing: *referred by reading specialist*

	year	month	day
Date of Test	*2000*	*8*	*29*
Date of Birth	*1991*	*5*	*7*
Chronological Age	*9*	*3*	*22*
	year	month	day*

Do not round months up by one if days exceed 15.

Confidence Interval Values

Age	Confidence Level	
	90%	95%
2	±7	±8
3-11	±5	±6
12-18	±4	±5

TEST RESULTS

Raw Score	Standard Score	Confidence Interval: *95*%	Percentile Rank	Age Equivalent
97	*106*	*100 — 112*	*66*	*10-0*

Scaled score: 11

Standard Score	Expressive Vocabulary	Receptive Vocabulary	Percentile Rank
145			>99
140			>99
135			99
130			98
125			95
120			91
115		X	84
110			75
105	X		63
100			50
95			37
90			25
85			16
80			9
75			5
70			2
65			1
60			<1
55			<1

Comparison of Expressive and Receptive Vocabulary

Expressive (EOWPVT) Standard Score	*106*
Receptive (ROWPVT) Standard Score	*114*
Difference	*-8*
Statistical Significance*	*.05*
Percent of Sample with this Difference*	*>25%*

*See test manual for values.

Comments: *Jane's expressive and receptive vocabulary scores are within the average ability range (within one standard deviation of the mean).*

Academic Therapy Publications, 20 Commercial Blvd., Novato, CA 94949
800 422-7249 • FAX 415 883-3720 • www.ATPub.com • Reorder No. 8137-1

Summary of Instructions for Test Administration

Refer to the test manual for complete instructions.

General Instructions: Say: "I am going to show you some pictures, and I want you to tell me the word that names each picture or group of pictures."

Administration: Administer the example items to all examinees. Begin with the test plate that corresponds to the examinee's chronological age. If a basal is not established on the first eight (8) items administered, work backward until eight (8) consecutive correct responses are made. Then work forward until six (6) consecutive incorrect responses are made.

Scoring: Write down the response to each item. Put a slash mark through the item number for an incorrect response. Responses that include the root word are scored as correct. The presence or absence of an inflectional ending, which indicates number or tense, has no bearing on the acceptability of a response.

Basal: Established by eight (8) consecutive correct responses.

Ceiling: Established by six (6) consecutive incorrect responses.

Recording Responses: Record in the space after each word all responses whether right or wrong. This will prevent the examinee from making an analysis of his or her success or failure.

Prompts: Use a prompt for each item. This identifies the elements in the illustration to which the examinee is to respond. For the majority of items, the prompt "*What's this?*" is appropriate. For items in which a different prompt should be used, the prompt is listed with the item. If a prompt is not listed with the item, the prompt "*What's this?*" should be used.

Cues: For responses indicating that the examinee is not attending to the appropriate feature of the illustration, use a verbal cue that directs the examinee's attention. Different cues are used for object, action, and concept items. Refer to the manual for instructions and examples of appropriate cues.

Item Starting Points

Age	Item	Age	Item
2-0–2-11	1	8-0–8-11	60
3-0–3-11	10	9-0–10-11	70
4-0–4-11	20	11-0–12-11	80
5-0–5-11	30	13-0–14-11	90
6-0–6-11	40	15-0–18-11	100
7-0–7-11	50		

Obtaining a Raw Score

Ceiling item*	*120*
Minus errors	– *23*
Raw Score	*97*

Transfer the Raw Score to page 1.

The prompt, "*What's this?*" should be used with each item unless another prompt is listed with the item.

EXAMPLES

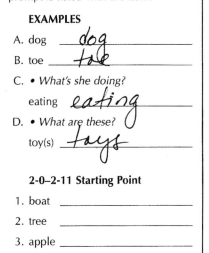

A. dog _*dog*_

B. toe _*toe*_

C. • *What's she doing?*

   eating _*eating*_

D. • *What are these?*

   toy(s) _*toys*_

2-0–2-11 Starting Point

1. boat _____

2. tree _____

3. apple _____

4. • *What are these?*

   eye(s) _____

5. kitty/kitten/cat _____

6. (tele)phone _____

7. bird _____

8. scissor(s) _____

9. bus _____

3-0–3-11 Starting Point

10. swing _____

11. bike/bicycle _____

12. sofa/couch _____

13. plane/airplane/jet _____

14. book _____

15. duck _____

16. train _____

17. leaf _____

18. watch _____

19. truck _____

4-0–4-11 Starting Point

20. computer _____

21. corn _____

22. • *What's he doing?*

   paint(er/ing) _____

23. kite _____

24. wagon _____

25. chicken/rooster/hen _____

26. cup _____

27. basket _____

* If more than one ceiling or basal is established, use the lowest ceiling and the highest basal.

28. ear _____

29. wheel _____

5-0-5-11 Starting Point

30. cloud(s) _____

31. tiger _____

32. smoke _____

33. mermaid _____

34. • What word names all of these?

animal(s) _____

35. wall _____

36. penguin _____

37. • What word names all of these?

bug(s)/insect(s) _____

38. starfish/sea star _____

39. • What word names all of these?

clothe(s/ing) _____

6-0-6-11 Starting Point

40. tire _____

41. bridge _____

42. • What are these?

suitcase(s)/luggage/baggage/

bag(s) _____

43. skateboard _____

44. • What are these?

footprint(s) _____

45. • What word names all of these?

fruit _____

46. skeleton _____

47. • What word names all of these?

light(s) _____

48. (fish) tank/

aquarium _____

49. raccoon _____

7-0-7-11 Starting Point

50. • What word names all of these?

food _____

51. antler(s)/horn(s) _____

52. • What's he doing?

sew(ing) _____

---

53. • What word names all of these? ⑥

drink(s)/beverage(s)/refreshment(s)

_____

54. fireplace _____

55. dentist _____

56. • What word names all of these?

furniture _____

57. cactus _____

58. • What are these?

statue(s) _____

59. binocular(s) _____

8-0-8-11 Starting Point

60. wrench _____

61. • What word names all of these?

(musical) instrument(s)

_____

62. pineapple _____

63. stool _____

64. • What word names all of these?

fly(ing)/flight _____

④ 65. telescope _____

66. goat _goat_

67. • What word names all of these?

mail _mail_

68. ostrich _ostrich_

③ 69. rectangle/

parallelogram _rectangle_

9-0-10-11 Starting Point ①

70. leopard/jaguar/

cheetah _leopard_

71. compass _compass_

72. shield _shield_

73. • What word names all of these?

write(ing)/

⑤ draw(ing) _writing_

② 74. lobster/crawfish/

crawdad _tarantula_

⑤ 75. thermometer _thermometer_

---

76. America/U.S.(A.)/United States

(of America) _America_

77. saddle _saddle_

78. trumpet _horn/trumpet_

79. wheelbarrow _wheelbarrow_

11-0-12-11 Starting Point

80. percent(age) _percent_

81. windmill _windmill_

82. paw _paw_

83. chess _chess_

84. tweezer(s) _pullers_

85. • What word names all of these?

time _time_

86. stadium/arena _football game_

87. stump _stump_

88. • What word names all of these?

cut(ting)/sharp _cutters_

89. • What are these?

pyramid(s) _tents_

13-0-14-11 Starting Point

90. • What are they doing?

skydive(er(s)/ing)/para-

chute(er(s)/ing) _skydiving_

91. • What word names all of these?

measure(er(s)/ing) _measurer_

92. reptile(s) _reptiles_

93. celery _broccoli_

94. • What word names all of these?

transportation/travel/

vehicle(s) _travel_

95. • What are these?

spring(s) _don't know_

96. banjo _banjo_

97. graph/chart _map_

98. boomerang _don't know_

99. greenhouse _store_

15-0-18-11 Starting Point

100. dock/pier _dock_

101. hoof _horse foot_

Basal: 8 consecutive correct responses. Ceiling: 6 consecutive incorrect responses.

102. water _letters_

103. • *What word names all of these?*
direction(s) _signs_

104. microscope _microscope_

105. hammock _hammock_

106. Africa _island_

107. • *What word names all of these?*
feeling(s)/emotion(s)/expression(s)/
reaction(s) _faces_

108. • *What word names all of these?*
seasoning(s)/
spice(s) _jars_

109. funnel _funnel_

110. battery _don't know_

111. scroll _paper_

112. clarinet _clarinet_

113. scale(s)/balance _weighers_

114. bulldozer _bulldozer_

115. • *What word names all of these?*
appliance(s) _electric_

116. hexagon _octagon_

117. column/pillar _holder_

118. reel _motor_

119. stethoscope _doctor thing_

⑦ 120. hourglass _don't know_

121. • *What's she doing?*
hurdle(er/ing) _____

122. • *What are these?*
monument(s)/
memorial(s) _____

123. anvil _____

124. otter _____

125. kayak _____

126. clamp _____

127. • *What word names all of these?*
rodent(s) _____

128. • *What word names all of these?*
communication/
information _____

129. • *What word names all of these?*
symbol(s)/sign(s) _____

130. beret _____

131. sphinx _____

132. • *What word names all of these?*
fungus(i/es) _____

133. tripod _____

134. • *What word names all of these?*
percussion _____

135. protractor _____

136. stirrup _____

137. • *What are these?*
hieroglyphic(s) _____

138. • *What are these?*
clef(s) _____

139. parallelogram/
rhomboid _____

140. squeegee _____

141. thermostat _____

142. beaker _____

143. • *What word names all of these?*
poultry/fowl _____

144. yoke _____

145. observatory _____

146. prescription _____

147. tine/prong _____

148. metronome _____

149. abacus _____

150. silhouette _____

151. filament _____

152. thistle _____

153. • *What word names all of these?*
gauge(s)/meter(s) _____

154. • *What's he doing?*
survey(or/ing) _____

155. candelabra _____

156. sickle _____

157. pommel/horn _____

158. • *What word names all of these?*
invertebrate(s) _____

159. tangent _____

160. monocular _____

161. scarab _____

162. sphere _____

163. trowel _____

164. shard _____

165. sextant _____

166. caster _____

167. outrigger _____

168. louver _____

169. plinth _____

170. dolmen _____

Basal: 8 consecutive correct responses. Ceiling: 6 consecutive incorrect responses.

Key to Example

1. (Item 70) Starting point.
2. (Item 74) Missed item before a basal of 8 is established.
3. (Item 69) Items 69 and below are administered to establish a basal of 8.
4. (Items 66–73) Basal of 8 established.
5. (Item 75) Testing resumes with the item following the item that indicated the need to work backward.
6. (Items 76–83) A second basal of 8 is established. Because this is the highest basal, it is used for scoring. Item 76 is the basal item. Items below item 76 are counted correct in calculating the raw score.
7. (Items 115–120) A ceiling of 6 is established. Item 120 is the ceiling item.

Section 4:

Interpretation

A raw score by itself provides little information about an examinee's level of performance. When the raw score is compared to some standard, it then becomes meaningful. Derived scores are provided to the user of the EOW-PVT so that an examinee's performance can be compared to a defined norms group. The derived scores serve a dual purpose. First, they indicate the examinee's relative standing compared to the normative sample and thus permit an evaluation of the individual's performance in reference to other persons. Second, they provide measures that permit a comparison of the individual's performance on the EOWPVT to performance on other tests.

When a raw score is obtained and the examinee's chronological age is computed, three types of derived scores are typically of interest: standard scores, percentile ranks, and age equivalents. Other widely used derived scores (NCEs, scaled scores, T-scores, and stanines) are also available.

Obtaining Derived Scores

Derived scores are listed in the norms tables found in Appendix D, Tables D.1 through D.3. Scores from these tables should be entered in the Test Results box on the front page of the record form. The procedure for converting raw scores to derived scores is described below. Examples correspond to the completed portion of the record form shown in Figure 4.1.

Standard Scores

To determine the standard score, turn to Table D.1 and locate the column that represents the appropriate chronological age level and the row corresponding to the raw score. The standard score is located where the row and column intersect.

For example, if a child whose chronological age is 9 years and 3 months obtains a raw score of 97, the corresponding standard score is 106.

Note that standard scores range from 55–145. When an individual's raw score falls below the standard score limit, it should be recorded as <55. Similarly, if the raw score is beyond the standard score limit of 145, it should be recorded as >145.

Record the standard score in the appropriate space in the Test Results box on the front page of the record form. Then, for a visual reference, plot the standard score on the chart below the Test Results box. The left hand column of the chart shows standard scores. Place an "X" next to the corresponding standard score value in the column labeled "Expressive Vocabulary."

FIGURE 4.1
Test Results Example

TEST RESULTS									
Raw Score	97	Standard Score	106	Confidence Interval: 95%	100 — 112	Percentile Rank	66	Age Equivalent	10-0

Scaled Score : 11

Standard Score Confidence Intervals

The standard score confidence interval is determined by referring to the table labeled "Confidence Interval Values" on the front page of the record form. This table shows the value that should be subtracted from and added to the obtained standard score. These values are provided for two levels of confidence: 90 and 95 percent. Follow these steps to establish the confidence interval:

1. Decide on the level of confidence required for the purpose of testing and record the confidence level on the line in the heading "Confidence Interval:___%" on the record form.
2. From the Confidence Interval Values table, find the value for the examinee's age level for the selected confidence level.
3. Subtract that value from the obtained standard score and record it on the record form.
4. Add the same value to the obtained standard score and record that value on the record form.

For example, the value for the 95 percent confidence level for a 9-year-old is 6. The confidence interval for a standard score of 106 is recorded as 100–112 (106–6=100; 106+6=112). (For standard scores recorded as <55 or >145, use the values 55 and 145 to determine the confidence interval.)

After entering the confidence interval on the record form, plot it on the chart by drawing a line from the lowest value in the confidence interval to the highest value. The line should be drawn through the "X" that represents the obtained standard score so that the confidence interval surrounding the obtained score can be easily seen.

Percentile Ranks and Other Related Scores

Because standard scores are normally distributed, a single table is provided for determining percentile ranks for all age levels. Turn to Table D.2 to obtain the percentile rank corresponding to a standard score. Other widely used derived scores are also located in this table, and the examiner may want to list one or more of these corresponding values in the space provided on the record form below the Test Results box.

For example, for an examinee who obtains a standard score of 106, the percentile rank is 66. If scaled scores were also of interest, that value would be read from the same row as the standard score and the percentile rank. For a standard score of 106, the corresponding scaled score is 11.

Age Equivalents

An age equivalent may be obtained by turning to Table D.3 and locating the age equivalent that corresponds to the raw score.

For example, if a child whose chronological age is 9 years and 3 months obtains a raw score of 97, the corresponding age equivalent is 10-0.

Interpreting Derived Scores

It is important that the user of the EOWPVT understand the meaning of the various derived scores. Before discussing the score characteristics, a few issues essential to the interpretation of the EOWPVT scores should be mentioned. First, it is important to remember that the behavior measured by the EOWPVT is expressive vocabulary. While there is clearly a relationship between vocabulary and general ability, tests of vocabulary do not provide a direct index of general ability, and inferences concerning general ability should be made with caution. Second, derived scores provide a means of comparing an individual's performance to a defined norms group. Such comparisons are of meaning only when we are interested in an individual's performance relative to a population that closely resembles that of the standardization sample. It is important that interpretations are made within this context. Finally, the user of the EOWPVT or any other educational or psychological test should be aware that obtained scores reflect errors of measurement. It is therefore important that the Standard Error of Measurement (SEM) is considered when interpreting the various EOWPVT scores and when making comparisons of EOWPVT performance across individuals or to performance on other assessments.

Table 4.1 shows the interrelationships of the various derived scores, which correspond to stanines, and contains a verbal description associated with each of these score ranges.

TABLE 4.1
Comparison of the Interrelationships of Derived Scores

Verbal Description	Range of Standard Scores	Range of Percentile Ranks	Stanines
Superior 4%	126 and above	96 and above	9
Above Average 19%	118–125 111–117	89–95 77–88	8 7
Average 54%	104–110 96–103 89–95	60–76 40–59 23–39	6 5 4
Below Average 19%	82–88 73–81	11–22 4–10	3 2
Low 4%	72 and below	Below 4	1

Standard Error of Measurement

Because a degree of imprecision may be associated with any type of measurement, an obtained score may differ from an individual's "true" score. An obtained score should be considered as representing a possible range of scores rather than a precise measurement. The SEM can be used to predict the range of fluctuation likely to occur in a single individual's score as a result of irrelevant, chance factors. Table 7.4, page 67, presents the SEM for raw scores and standard scores for each age level.

When interpreting a particular score, if plus or minus 1.65 SEMs is added to the score, the 90 percent confidence interval is obtained. This confidence interval is the score range in which there is a 90 percent probability that the individual's true score is contained within its limits. If plus or minus 1.96 SEMs is added to the score, the associated probability is 95 percent. Using the SEM, confidence intervals associated with other probabilities can be calculated (see Anastasi & Urbina, 1997).

It should be clear to the user of the EOWPVT that small differences between scores may represent errors of measurement rather than actual differences in ability. Small differences between scores of individuals, therefore, should not be considered meaningful.

Standard Scores

A standard score indicates the extent to which an individual's EOWPVT performance deviates from the average performance of those at the same age level. Tables for standard scores corresponding to raw scores are provided for ages 2–4 in one-month intervals, for ages 5–10 in two-month intervals, ages 11–13 in three-month intervals, and for ages 14–18 in four-month intervals. The distribution of standard scores for each level has a mean of 100 and a standard deviation of 15. This means that if an individual's rank relative to others remains constant from year to year, the standard score will also remain constant. Standard scores represent equal units of measurement and are comparable to standard scores from other tests, provided that a mean of 100 and a standard deviation of 15 is used and that the norm groups are similar. In particular, a standard score obtained on the EOWPVT can be compared directly to a standard score obtained on the *Receptive One-Word Picture Vocabulary Test* (ROWPVT) since both tests provide norms based on the same group.

Percentile Ranks

Percentile ranks provide an index of an individual's relative standing in reference to other individuals at that age level. A percentile rank of 50 represents average performance; it is the median value. Percentiles can be regarded as ranks in a group of 100—the lower the percentile, the poorer the individual's standing; the higher the percentile, the greater the individual's standing. An individual who scores at the 65th percentile, for example, has performed as well or better than 65 percent of the individuals at that age level in the norms group.

Percentiles should not be confused with familiar percentage scores, which indicate the percentage of items correct. Percentiles are derived scores that refer to the percentage of persons in the norm group at a particular age level that achieved a particular raw score. Unlike standard scores, percentile ranks do not represent equal units of measurement. The difference in ability between the 45th and 50th percentile rank, for example, is small compared to the difference between the 90th and the 95th percentile ranks. When an index of rank or relative standing within an age level is required, percentile ranks are appropriate.

Age Equivalents

An age equivalent is a familiar and convenient index of an individual's EOWPVT performance. An age equivalent provides information about an individual's relative standing in reference to the entire norms group. For example, if an individual, regardless of chronological age, obtains a raw score of 97, Table D.3 shows that the individual's age equivalent is 10–0. This indicates that EOWPVT performance was the same as that of the average ten-year-old in the norms group.

Because equal intervals of age do not correspond to equal units of ability, comparisons using this index should be made with caution. Age equivalents are best thought of as ranks that represent relative standing. When comparing scores of individuals or groups, or comparing performance across tests, standard scores are the preferred index of performance.

Comparing Expressive and Receptive Vocabulary Performance

Since the EOWPVT and the ROWPVT have been conormed, performance from one test can be compared directly to performance on the other test. When such comparisons are made, errors of measurement must be taken into account so that small discrepancies in performance, which may be due to errors of measurement rather than actual differences in ability, are not viewed as significant. Additionally, the frequency with which such discrepancies occurred in the standardization sample should be considered.

To aid in the interpretation of differences between the two test scores, the score differences required for significance at several levels of confidence are provided for each age level in Table D.4. The frequency of occurrence of different discrepancy values within the norms group is presented in Table D.5.

When the EOWPVT and ROWPVT have both been administered to an individual, the following steps can be taken to make a comparison between expressive and receptive vocabulary performance.

1. Refer to the box on the front page of the record form and write the EOWPVT and ROWPVT standard scores in the spaces provided.
2. Subtract the ROWPVT from the EOWPVT score to obtain the difference.
3. Refer to Table D.4 to obtain the level of statistical significance of the difference. The table lists absolute values so ignore the sign of the difference (e.g., –8 should be considered 8). If the difference is not significant, write "ns" on the record form and skip step 4.
4. Refer to Table D.5 to obtain the percent of the standardization sample that had a difference of the observed magnitude.

For example, for a nine-year-old having an EOWPVT standard score of 106 and an ROWPVT standard score of 114, a difference of –8 is obtained. The absolute value of –8 is 8. Table D.4 indicates that the magnitude of this difference is significant at the .05 level. Table D.5 indicates that a difference of this magnitude occurred in more than 25 percent of the standardization sample. Although the difference is significant, it would be concluded that this is not a meaningful difference since differences of this magnitude are common. Figure 4.2 shows how the record form would be completed for this example. If a significant difference is found and Table D.5 indicates that the magnitude of the difference is relatively rare—that is, it is found in only 1 or 5 percent of the sample— then, in most cases, further evaluation should be considered. For each examinee, the importance of the difference must be evaluated in light of the individual's overall performance and the reason for testing.

FIGURE 4.2
Example of Comparison of Obtained EOWPVT and ROWPVT Standard Scores

Comparison of Expressive and Receptive Vocabulary	
Expressive (EOWPVT) Standard Score	*106*
Receptive (ROWPVT) Standard Score	*114*
Difference	*– 8*
Statistical Significance*	*.05*
Percent of Sample with this Difference*	*25%*

*See test manual for values.

Differences can occur with either expressive or receptive vocabulary performance being significantly and meaningfully below performance on the other test.

Expressive Lower than Receptive Performance. While ROWPVT performance requires an individual to recognize an illustration that depicts the meaning of a word, the EOWPVT has the added task requirement of retrieving the word from memory that best describes an object, action, or concept, presented in an illustration. Lower EOWPVT performance could mean that the individual has word retrieval difficulties that affect the extent of his or her speaking vocabulary relative to the extent of the individual's hearing vocabulary.

Receptive Lower than Expressive Performance. Lower ROWPVT performance could mean that the individual has difficulties with aspects of the task requirements of the test that differ from those of the EOWPVT. Because the ROWPVT is a multiple-choice test, the facility with which an individual is able to deduce an answer, when the answer is not clearly known, is likely to have a more substantial effect on test performance than it would on the EOWPVT. The ROWPVT also requires the individual to hear a word and to review four illustrations in determining a response to each item. Because of the difference in the task format, the ROWPVT is a more perceptually-demanding test than the EOWPVT, and auditory or visual difficulties may account for this type of difference. With a more complex stimulus than that presented on the EOWPVT, a higher level of concentration is required, and examinees who lack focus or are easily distracted could show lower ROW-PVT performance.

When significant and meaningful differences are obtained between the EOWPVT and the ROWPVT, probable reasons for the difference should be identified through reference to other information known about the individual including results from other tests.

Making Comparisons to Other Tests

When comparing EOWPVT performance to other assessment results, standard scores are the preferred index of performance. Valid comparisons can only be made when the standard score scales have the same mean and standard deviation and when the norms are based on similar reference groups. Standard scores for the EOWPVT have a mean of 100 and a standard deviation of 15. Many tests use this same scale. When tests use other scales, such as normal curve equivalents (NCEs) or scaled scores, all test results need to be transformed to a common scale. Table D.3 provides a conversion of standard scores to a number of widely used scales.

Errors of measurement also need to be taken into account when making score comparisons. Measurement textbooks, such as Anastasi and Urbina (1997), provide methods for making such comparisons.

Section 5:
Development

This section details the procedures followed in selecting items that comprise the final form of the EOWPVT. A discussion of the item selection procedures is followed by a summary of the various item analyses that were conducted, which includes an analysis of item bias.

Initial Item Selection

Items appearing in this edition of the EOWPVT include those from previous editions of the lower and upper levels of the test as well as several new items. For the first edition of the test, an effort was made to obtain a list of common words that children learn and use at an early age. To obtain such a list, letters were sent to 435 parents of children ranging in age from 18 months to 2 years. The letters asked the parents to report, via a questionnaire, words used by their child and at what age each word was first used. Words that were reported as frequently known by young children were chosen for inclusion on the preliminary form of the test. Other words for the previous editions were chosen because individuals are commonly exposed to the words in the home, community, or school environments.

From the original 176 items from the previous editions of the two levels of the EOWPVT, 32 items were deleted for one of several reasons. These reasons included the possibility of an item being culturally biased, representing an anachronism, being ambiguous in terms of ease of recognition, or otherwise problematic. Forty-six new items were added. Items were added at various difficulty levels to replace deleted items, and additional easy and difficult items were added to ensure that the test would assess a wide range of ability. New items were selected from a number of vocabulary sources. The sources included *The Educator's Word Frequency Guide* (Zeno et al., 1995), *The Reading Teacher's Book of Lists* (Fry et al., 1993), the *EDL Core Vocabularies in Reading, Mathematics, Science, and Social Studies* (Taylor et al., 1989), *Basic Reading Vocabularies* (Harris & Jacobson, 1982), *The Living Word Vocabulary* (Dale & O'Rourke, 1981), and the *Computational Analysis of Present-Day American English* (Kucera & Francis, 1967). Items were selected that could be illustrated, that would yield a one-word response, and that had few responses that could be considered correct. Definitions of acceptable answers were verified in *Merriam-Webster's Collegiate Dictionary, Tenth Edition* (1999).

The preliminary form included a total of 190 items, four of which were sample items. All items were illustrated in a common style. For the final form of the test, subtle color was added to increase the appeal of the artwork.

For the current edition, several decisions were made that affect the administration and scoring of each item. These decisions were based on test user comments received since the first publication of the test, recommendations made from test user surveys, discussion groups held to specifically address administration issues, and observation of administration of the test. From this information the following decisions regarding item administration and scoring were made:

- Prompts would be given with each item to focus examinees on the intent of the item and thereby reduce item ambiguity.
- Cues would be given when an examinee gives a response that indicates that he or she is focusing on the wrong aspect of the item.
- A response would be counted correct if the examinee identified the root of the word; lexical endings (i.e., endings that denote plurals or verb tense) would not have a bearing on scoring.

The 190 items and revised administration and scoring rules were used for pilot testing, which is described below.

Pilot Test

A pilot test was conducted in October and November 1998 to establish item difficulties and to examine item validity and other test characteristics. Item difficulties needed to be established so that items from three sources—the EOWPVT Lower Level, the EOWPVT Upper-Extension, and the new items—could be combined into a single form and arranged in order of difficulty. This would simplify administration for standardization.

The pilot test form consisted of three parts: Part 1 contained items retained from the EOWPVT Lower Level; Part 2 contained items retained from the EOWPVT Upper-Extension; and Part 3 consisted of the new items. The original item sequences, which were based on increasing item difficulty, were maintained for Parts 1 and 2. For Part 3, item order was based on a structured rating of the perceived difficulty of the items, which proved to be an accurate method of determining item sequence (rank order correlation of initial/final order: .95). Basal and ceilings of eight consecutive items were used for Parts 1 and 2, and a basal and ceiling of ten was used for Part 3.

The pilot test was conducted at five schools in California with 154 students whose ages ranged from 2 through 18. All students were administered each of the three test parts. The *Receptive One-Word Picture Vocabulary Test* (ROWPVT) was administered at the same time. The demographics of the pilot test sample are listed in Table 5.1.

TABLE 5.1
Demographic Characteristics of the Pilot Test Sample (*N*=154)

Characteristics	N	Percentage
Race/Ethnicity:		
Asian	22	14.3
Black	9	5.8
Hispanic	15	9.7
White	106	68.8
Other	2	1.3
Gender:		
Female	74	48.1
Male	80	51.9
Parent Education Level:		
Grade 11 or less	4	2.6
High School	16	10.4
1–3 Years College	45	29.2
4+ Years College	89	57.8
Educational Classification:		
Regular Ed.	154	100.0

Initial Item Analysis

Examinee responses that had been scored incorrect were first screened to determine whether additional responses should be counted correct. When additional acceptable responses were identified, items were rescored.

Analyses based on both Classical Test Theory (CTT) and Item Response Theory (IRT) were conducted. The CTT analyses involved the calculation for each item of item difficulty (the proportion of individuals passing an item), item discrimination (the biserial correlation of item performance with the raw score), and the item reliability index (this index indicates the amount of unique variance that the item contributes to the raw score). A one-parameter IRT analysis was also conducted. This analysis, often referred to as a Rasch analysis, yielded item calibrations and goodness-of-fit data. Phi coefficients were also calculated between demographic characteristics and item scores as a preliminary means of examining potential item bias.

Based on these analyses, four items were eliminated, and the remaining items were arranged in order of increasing difficulty. Item order was based on item difficulty data obtained from both the CTT analysis and the item calibrations from the Rasch analysis. This sequence of items served as the standardization edition and contained more items than would be included on the final form of the test.

Second Item Analysis

During collection of the normative data, a second item analysis was conducted. The first part of this analysis involved repeating the CTT and IRT analyses that were performed on the pilot edition. The second part of the analysis was concerned with identifying items that might be biased toward a particular group of individuals. As a result of these analyses, the items that would comprise the final form of the test were identified.

CTT and IRT Analyses

For this analysis a sample of 510 examinees was selected from the protocols received from the standardization study. This sample was comprised of 30 individuals at each one-year age level, from 2 through 18. Individuals within each group of 30 were randomly selected from the protocols available at that point in the study (2,912) to match the population characteristics of the U.S. in regard to geographic region, race/ethnicity, gender, residence, level of parent education, and educational classification. Table 5.2 shows the demographic characteristics for this sample.

Selection of a sample representative of the U.S. population across age levels provided an accurate means of evaluating the sensitivity of items across the full range of ability. This information was critical for determining which items to delete from the test— all else being equal, items sharing similar difficulty to many other items were considered better candidates for deletion than items sharing similar difficulty values with relatively fewer items. Item difficulty was evaluated by examining percent passing along with Rasch item calibrations. Item statistics, such as item discrimination, reliability indexes, and goodness-of-fit statistics, were also reconsidered at this time.

Item Bias

Item bias studies were conducted to provide a test that would be fair in evaluating the speaking vocabulary of individuals with various backgrounds. This process involved consideration of qualitative information provided by individuals participating in the standardization study and a review by a panel of individuals of diverse cultural background. This information was taken together with a quantitative analysis of bias that detects differential item functioning.

TABLE 5.2
Demographic Characteristics of the Second Item Analysis Sample (N=510)

Characteristics	N	Percentage	Percentage of School-Age Population
Region:			
Northeast	92	18.0	19.4
North Central	124	24.3	23.4
South	180	35.3	35.1
West	114	22.4	22.1
Race/Ethnicity:			
Asian	14	2.7	3.5
Black	60	11.8	12.1
Hispanic	47	9.2	11.0
White	387	75.9	72.7
Other	2	0.4	0.7
Gender:			
Female	255	50.0	48.9
Male	255	50.0	51.1
Parent Education:			
Grade 11 or less	84	16.5	17.5
High School	162	31.8	33.8
1–3 Years College	126	24.7	24.5
4+ Years College	138	27.0	24.2
Residence:			
Urban	409	80.2	75.2
Rural	101	19.8	24.8
Educational Classification:			
Regular Ed.	469	92.0	91.0
Special Ed.	41	8.0	9.0

Source: Population data: U.S. Bureau of the Census, 1998; Educational Classification data: Department of Education, 1995.

Item Review. All examiners in the standardization study were encouraged to identify items that might be biased or problematic in any way. This information was reviewed and summarized for use in identifying potentially biased items. Additionally, a number of individuals representing various race and ethnic groups and community types reviewed items and identified those that they felt depicted individuals inappropriately or reinforced stereotypes or items that might be easier or more difficult for a particular group. The cultural review panel included individuals representing Asian, Black, Hispanic, and Native American backgrounds as well as urban and rural communities. (A list of the individuals participating in this cultural review appears in Appendix B.)

Differential Item Functioning Analysis. To assess item bias quantitatively, an analysis of differential item functioning was performed using the Mantel-Haenzel procedure (Nandakumar et al., 1993). This procedure was used because it provides stable results even with relatively small sample sizes.

Differential item functioning occurs when individuals from one group having the same level of ability as a second group find an item more or less difficult. To detect differential item functioning, contrasts were made between groups based on gender (male/female), residence (urban/rural), and race/ethnicity (Black/White, Hispanic/White, Other/White). The number of individuals participating in this analysis was 2,945. Table 5.3 shows the number of individuals in each subgroup.

TABLE 5.3
Number of Examinees in Subgroups Used for the
Analysis of Differential Item Functioning
(N=2,945)

Characteristics	N
Race/Ethnicity:	
Black	483
Hispanic	203
White	2,150
Other	109
Gender:	
Female	1,579
Male	1,366
Residence:	
Urban	2,231
Rural	714

In each contrast individuals were assigned to one of five ability levels, based on their obtained EOWPVT raw score. The Mantel-Haenzel statistic was then calculated for each item, corrected using Holland and Thayer's (1988) procedure, and evaluated for significance based on the chi-square statistic.

Item Selection

To select the items that would remain on the final form of the EOWPVT, item analysis and differential item functioning statistics were considered along with the comments made by examiners and the members of the cultural review panel. As a result, 12 items were eliminated from the test. The remaining items are highly discriminating, culturally balanced, and sensitive to a wide range of ability.

A review of the final items was then conducted to ensure that the test plates present fair representation of the gender and race and ethnic makeup of the nation. The balance of these characteristics in the final test plates is as follows: gender (female, 48%; male, 53%), race/ethnicity (Black, 16%; Hispanic, 21%; White, 42%; Other, 16%).

Final Item Analysis

Following selection of the standardization sample (see a description of the sample in the following section), an item analysis was performed based on the 170 final test items. All tests were rescored using a basal of eight consecutive correct responses and a ceiling of six consecutive incorrect responses (examiners had obtained a ceiling of eight). Because a sufficiently large sample size was available, item analysis statistics were calculated at the age group level as well as for the total sample. The information presented here is a summary of selected statistics from that analysis.

While the previous item analyses focused on the full age continuum of the test, it is of interest to examine how the final form of the test functions at each age level. Item difficulty and discrimination information by age level can show (1) whether the overall sequence of items, which was based on the item difficulty of the full age range of the pilot test sample, is appropriate at each age level, (2) whether the items that comprise the range of those items typically administered* at each age level have acceptable levels of discrimination, and (3) whether the range of items administered at each age level is sufficiently broad to be sensitive to a range of performance.

Appropriate item order is critical to the efficient administration of the EOWPVT. The correlation of item difficulty to item order for the standardization sample as a whole is .99. Correlations were also calculated for each age group based on the range of items administered. Table 5.4 shows these correlations. The correlations across age groups range from .93 to .98 with a median of .96. For each age group, there is a strong relationship between item order and item difficulty. For a test such as the EOWPVT, which uses basals and ceilings to limit the number of items administered, this means that examinees are administered the items with maximum differentiating power for their ability level without having to have an excessive number of items administered that are too easy or too difficult.

Table 5.4 also shows the median item discrimination indexes for the items administered to examinees in each age group in the standardization sample. The item discrimination index is the biserial correlation of item performance to the total raw score, which provides an index of item discrimi-

---

*"Range of items administered" refers to the set of items that had variance for each age group. Items in which all individuals pass or fail an item do not have variance.

TABLE 5.4
Correlation of Item Difficulty with Item Order and Median Item Discrimination Index by Age Group

Age Group	Correlation of Item Order with Item Difficulty*	Median Item Discrimination Index
2	.93	.82
3	.93	.81
4	.96	.81
5	.97	.77
6	.97	.75
7	.98	.77
8	.96	.78
9	.96	.84
10	.96	.78
11	.95	.78
12	.95	.90
13	.94	.99
14	.93	.99
15–16	.96	.83
17–18	.94	.87
Median	.96	.81
All Ages	.99	.91

*Correlations are negative and minus signs are omitted.

nation that is independent of item difficulty (Henryssen, 1971). Inspection of the medians shows that the level of discrimination of items typically administered to examinees in each age group is consistently high. The median value for the total age range is .91. Median values across age groups range from .75 to .99 with an overall median of .81.

Figure 5.1 further characterizes the items that comprise the final form of the EOWPVT. This chart shows a line for each age group that represents the range of items that were administered to that group. The shaded box shows the range of items that have difficulty values between .20 and .80. Items within this range have maximum differentiating power for the particular age group. Finally, the chart shows a curve running across age groups that represents the smoothed medians.

The curve of the smoothed medians shows a steady increase in performance across age levels with smaller increments of increased performance with each ascending age level. The range of items with maximum differentiation and the range of items administered, as expected, closely track and are centered around the smoothed medians. Inspection of these ranges shows that the EOWPVT has relatively equal sensitivity across age levels with the lowest age level having the most restricted range of maximum differentiating items. Figure 5.1 also shows that there are limited floor and ceiling restrictions in the range of items administered, indicating that the range of item difficulties is sufficient for assessing individuals within the intended age range.

FIGURE 5.1
Range of Items Administered by Age Group

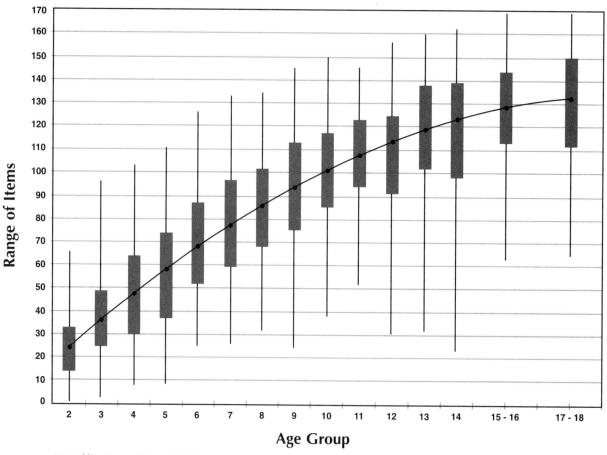

Vertical line: Range of items administered
Shaded box: Range of items with item difficulty values between .20 and .80
•: Smoothed median

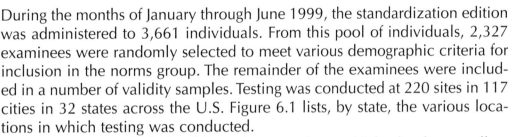

Section 6:

Standardization

During the months of January through June 1999, the standardization edition was administered to 3,661 individuals. From this pool of individuals, 2,327 examinees were randomly selected to meet various demographic criteria for inclusion in the norms group. The remainder of the examinees were included in a number of validity samples. Testing was conducted at 220 sites in 117 cities in 32 states across the U.S. Figure 6.1 lists, by state, the various locations in which testing was conducted.

Institutions included public, private, and parochial schools as well as private practices. Additionally, some examinees were tested in their homes. (For a listing of the institutions and individuals participating in the standardization study, see Appendix B.)

Test sites were obtained by contacting individuals from Academic Therapy Publications' customer files who had purchased the EOWPVT or the ROWPVT. This resulted in the participation of 245 examiners. The vast majority of these individuals were speech-language pathologists; others included school psychologists, educational specialists, and graduate students supervised by an instructor.

Several locations served as primary test sites. At these sites one individual coordinated the efforts of a group of test administrators, and the site was responsible for collecting data across age levels. Primary sites were located in each geographic region: Northeast—New Bedford, MA; Howell, NJ; North Central—Wichita, KS; Lennox, SD; Wakonda, SD; Milwaukee, WI; South—Clanton, AL; Miami, FL; Milledgeville, GA; Saxe, VA; West—Oroville, CA; Shiprock, NM.

Data Collection

Examiners were provided with test materials and instructed to select students randomly from regular classrooms. They were also encouraged to

FIGURE 6.1
Standardization Locations

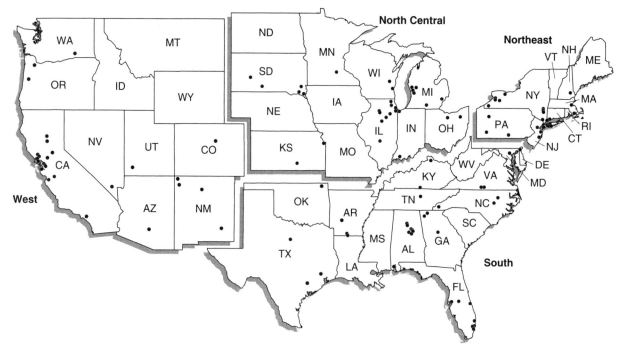

Northeast
Connecticut
Orange
Stamford
Massachusetts
Boston
New Bedford
New Hampshire
Manchester
New Jersey
Howell
Milltown
Shrewsbury
New York
Albertson
Alexander
Amherst
Brooklyn
Buffalo
Commack
Oceanside
Poughkeepsie
Red Hook
Rifton
Rochester
Sayville
Sherman
Tappan
Pennsylvania
Franklin
New Oxford
Perryopolis

North Central
Illinois
Chicago
East Moline
Fulton
Lexington
Normal
Norridge
Oakbrook Terrace
Pleasant Plains
Pontiac
Skokie
Indiana
East Chicago
Evansville
Kansas
Kansas City
Wichita
Michigan
Clinton
Fruitport
Hillsdale
Muskegon
Ravenna
Spring Lake
Minnesota
Delano
Ohio
Bedford
Fairview Park
South Dakota
Kyle

Lennox
Manderson
Rapid City
Wakonda
Wisconsin
Markesan
Milwaukee

South
Alabama
Birmingham
Clanton
Jemison
Maplesville
Mobile
Montevallo
Thorsby
Verbena
Arkansas
El Dorado
Hot Springs
Junction City
Delaware
New Castle
Florida
Delray
Hialeah
Lakeland
Miami
North Miami Beach
Sebastian
Tampa

Georgia
Blue Ridge
Ellijay
Milledgeville
Kentucky
Fort Thomas
Scottsville
Maryland
Belcamp
North Carolina
Cullowhee
Hillsborough
Louisburg
Oklahoma
Picher
Tennessee
Nashville
Texas
Crosby
Ferris
Schulenburg
Virginia
Charlotte Court
House
Saxe

West
Arizona
Phoenix
California
Berkeley
Castro Valley

Dixon
Dos Palos
Folsom
Magalia
Mill Valley
Novato
Oroville
Panorama City
Petaluma
Salinas
San Anselmo
San Lorenzo
San Mateo
Santa Rosa
Colorado
Littleton
New Mexico
Fruitland
Newcomb
Roswell
Shiprock
Nevada
Las Vegas
Oregon
Aloha
Hillsboro
Utah
Cedar City
Washington
Kennewick

administer the test to individuals representing a wide range of disability status. In addition to including a percentage of these examinees in the norms group, this data was used for validity studies.

All individuals were tested with the consent of their parent or guardian. Demographic information concerning age, gender, race/ethnicity, parent education level, and primary language was obtained from the parent or guardian. Examiners provided information concerning class placement, disability status, and residence (community size).

Examiners were asked to provide scores from other tests, when available, for use in validity studies. Additionally, retest data, for reliability studies, was provided by many examiners.

The EOWPVT and the ROWPVT were administered to each examinee. Examiners were instructed to administer the EOWPVT first. All EOWPVT tests were administered individually. Examiners scored items right or wrong as they administered the tests and did not calculate raw scores. Upon receipt of protocols, all data was screened for accuracy.

Examiners were encouraged to call the publisher if they had questions. In addition, phone and mail contact was maintained with examiners to ensure clarity of the administration procedures.

Black and White Versus Color Presentation

Although the final version of the EOWPVT provides full-color test plates, the majority of the sites in the standardization study were supplied with black and white test plates. Husband and Hayden (1996) compared students' performance on tests with black and white versus color presentation materials. Although students had a preference for color materials, no significant difference in performance was found. Based on this finding, it was assumed that performance would not be affected in using black and white versus color test plates in administering the EOWPVT.

To validate this assumption, 27 test sites were given color test plates. At these sites, 734 examinees were tested. A sample of 100 examinees was drawn from this group. Twenty individuals from each of the five age groupings used for norms stratification were randomly selected to match the U.S. population characteristics as closely as possible. A matched sample of examinees from sites using the black and white version was used for comparison. See Table 6.1 for a description of the color sample.

The black and white group had a mean raw score of 88.92 compared to a mean of 90.10 for the color group. A two-way analysis of variance with repeated measures on the color vs. black and white factor indicated that there were no significant differences in performance for any age group ($F_{14,85}$=1.24, p=.26) or for the group as a whole ($F_{1,85}$=.44, p=.51). This finding is in line with Husband and Hayden's research and supports the assumption that black and white and color test plates yield the same results.

TABLE 6.1
Demographic Characteristics of the Color Sample (N=100)

Characteristics	N	Percentage
Region:		
Northeast	15	15.0
North Central	37	37.0
South	29	29.0
West	19	19.0
Race/Ethnicity:		
Asian	2	2.0
Black	6	6.0
Hispanic	7	7.0
White	84	84.0
Other	1	1.0
Gender:		
Female	57	57.0
Male	43	43.0
Parent Education Level:		
Grade 11 or less	9	9.0
High School	26	26.0
1–3 Years College	26	26.0
4+ Years College	39	39.0
Residence		
Urban	80	80.0
Rural	20	20.0

Selected for the comparison of black and white to color presentation. (A second sample of 100 students who had been presented the black and white version were matched to this sample.)

Standardization Sample Demographic Characteristics

Norms for the EOWPVT were derived from the sample described in Tables 6.2 through 6.4. Individuals were randomly selected from the pool of 3,661 individuals tested. Only individuals whose primary language at home and school is English were included in the norms group. Table 6.2 compares the demographic characteristics of the total sample of 2,327 examinees to the characteristics of the U.S. population. Overall, the sample closely approximates the demographics of the U.S. population.

Table 6.3 shows the number of individuals tested in each of 15 age groups. Age groups for individuals ages 2 through 14 are in one-year intervals and in 2-year intervals for ages 15 through 18, where the pace of vocabulary development declines. The number of individuals tested is lowest at the

TABLE 6.2
Demographic Characteristics of the Standardization Sample

Characteristics	Percentage of Sample	Percentage of School-Age Population
Region:		
Northeast	18.7	19.4
North Central	24.3	23.4
South	35.0	35.1
West	22.0	22.1
Race/Ethnicity:		
Asian	2.3	3.5
Black	13.7	12.1
Hispanic	9.9	11.0
White	72.7	72.7
Other	1.4	0.7
Gender:		
Female	48.2	48.9
Male	51.8	51.1
Parent Education Level:		
Grade 11 or less	11.8	17.5
High School	32.7	33.8
1–3 Years College	26.7	24.5
4+ Years College	28.8	24.2
Residence:		
Urban	74.8	75.2
Rural	25.2	24.8
Disability Status:		
No Disability	89.9	91.0
Learning Disability	2.4	5.5
Speech-Language Disorder	5.7	2.3
Mentally Retarded	1.0	1.1
Other	1.0	0.1

2-0 through 2-11 age group and is highest particularly from ages 4 through 10, which are the ages at which this test is most frequently used.

Table 6.4 shows the stratification of the sample for each characteristic by age and compares these percentages to those of the U.S. population. These data show that the sample is representative of the U.S. population across the age range for which norms are provided.

U.S. population parameters for region, race/ethnicity, gender, parent education, and residence were obtained for school-age children from the *Statistical Abstract of the United States* (U.S. Bureau of the Census, 1998). Information regarding disability status is from the U.S. Department of Education (1995).

TABLE 6.3
Number of Examinees in the Standardization Sample by Age Group

Age Level	N	Age Level	N
2	60	10	182
3	105	11	133
4	209	12	132
5	205	13	131
6	221	14	103
7	228	15–16	124
8	184	17–18	119
9	191		
		Total	2,327

TABLE 6.4
Demographics of the Normative Sample Stratified by Age

Geographic Region by Age	Northeast		North Central		South		West	
Age (yrs.)	N	%	N	%	N	%	N	%
2-4	73	19.5	92	24.6	125	33.4	84	22.5
5-7	116	17.7	160	24.5	239	36.5	139	21.3
8-10	106	19.0	132	23.7	199	35.7	120	21.5
11-13	72	18.2	97	24.5	136	34.3	91	23.0
14-18	68	19.7	84	24.3	115	33.2	79	22.8
Total	435	18.7	565	24.3	814	35.0	513	22.0
Population		19.4		23.4		35.1		22.1

Race/Ethnicity by Age	Asian		Black		Hispanic		White		Other	
Age (yrs.)	N	%	N	%	N	%	N	%	N	%
2-4	8	2.1	54	14.4	18	4.8	291	77.8	3	0.8
5-7	15	2.3	96	14.7	68	10.4	465	71.1	10	1.5
8-10	21	3.8	83	14.9	66	11.8	379	68.0	8	1.4
11-13	3	0.8	45	11.4	46	11.6	300	75.8	2	0.5
14-18	7	2.0	41	11.8	32	9.2	257	74.3	9	2.6
Total	54	2.3	319	13.7	230	9.9	1,692	72.7	32	1.4
Population		3.5		12.1		11.0		72.7		0.7

Derivation of Norms

Raw scores, by themselves, provide little information about an individual's level of performance. To use the results from any test, raw scores need to be converted to a metric that provides a comparison to a standard. The most common and useful derived scores in educational assessment are stan-

TABLE 6.4—*Continued*

Gender by Age	Female			Male		
Age (yrs.)	*N*	%		*N*	%	
2-4	172	46.0		202	54.0	
5-7	310	47.4		344	52.6	
8-10	281	50.4		276	49.6	
11-13	184	46.5		212	53.5	
14-18	175	50.6		171	49.4	
Total	1,122	48.2		1,205	51.8	
Population		48.9			51.1	

Parent Education Level by Age	Grade 11 or less		High School Graduate		1-3 years college		4 or more years college	
Age (yrs.)	*N*	%	*N*	%	*N*	%	*N*	%
2-4	35	9.4	78	20.9	89	23.8	172	46.0
5-7	79	12.1	216	33.0	168	25.7	191	29.2
8-10	68	12.2	213	38.2	168	30.2	108	19.4
11-13	55	13.9	130	32.8	110	27.8	101	25.5
14-18	37	10.7	124	35.8	86	24.9	99	28.6
Total	274	11.8	761	32.7	621	26.7	671	28.8
Population		17.5		33.8		24.5		24.2

Residence by Age	Urban			Rural		
Age (yrs.)	*N*	%		*N*	%	
2-4	310	82.9		64	17.1	
5-7	431	65.9		223	34.1	
8-10	401	72.0		156	28.0	
11-13	329	83.1		67	16.9	
14-18	270	78.0		76	22.0	
Total	1,741	74.8		586	25.2	
Population		75.2			24.8	

dard scores, percentile ranks, and age equivalents. These are the types of scores derived for the EOWPVT. The methods for deriving these scores are described in this section.

Standard Scores

Standard scores are a type of transformed score in which the distribution of raw scores has been fitted to a normal distribution with a known mean and standard deviation. Standard scores describe a person's relative standing when performance is compared to a larger normative population. Because standard scores provide a common metric, they can be used to compare an individual's performance to other tests that also have derived scores, irrespective of the number of test items, as long as the norms for each test are based on normal distributions having the same mean and standard deviation.

Standard scores were derived using a method described by Angoff (1971), in which the cumulative frequency of each raw score was computed for each of the 15 age groups and the corresponding percentile ranks were plotted against the range of raw scores. The lines were then smoothed within and between age groups to remove irregularities due to sampling. For each age group new percentile ranks were read for each raw score. Corresponding z-scores were then obtained for each percentile rank, and standard scores were derived based on a distribution having a mean of 100 and standard deviation of 15.

The standard score values presented in Table D.1 in Appendix D were created by interpolating between the scores obtained for each of the age groups. For this purpose standard score distributions one year below the youngest group and one year above the oldest group were extrapolated. The tables show standard scores in one-month age intervals for ages 2-0 through 4-11, two-month age intervals for ages 5-0 through 10-11, three-month age intervals for ages 11-0 through 13-11, and four-month age intervals for ages 14-0 through 18-11.

Percentile Ranks and Other Derived Scores

A feature resulting from the normal transformation of raw scores is the consistency of all normative data. Because percentile ranks and many other types of derived scores correspond directly to the normal distribution, the same standard score obtained at any age level will always be associated with the same percentile rank or other derived score. Table D.2 in Appendix D shows the correspondence of percentile ranks to standard scores. Also provided in this table is a conversion from standard scores to other widely used derived scores (NCEs, T-scores, scaled scores, and stanines). These values were obtained by calculating the score, based on the mean and standard deviation of each scale, that corresponds to a given percentile rank.

Age Equivalents

Age equivalents correspond to the median raw scores obtained by individuals within a particular age group. The age equivalent tables presented in Table D.3 in Appendix D were created by plotting median raw scores for each age group against the midpoint of the age interval. The curve was then smoothed and the values for chronological ages corresponding to each raw score were read from the graph. Table 6.5 shows the smoothed medians and standard deviations for raw scores.

TABLE 6.5

Smoothed Median Raw Scores and Standard Deviations by Age Group

Age Group	N	Smoothed Median	Standard Deviation
2	60	24.25	10.04
3	105	36.25	14.01
4	209	47.25	15.07
5	205	57.75	14.69
6	221	67.75	15.03
7	228	77.00	15.81
8	184	85.50	14.76
9	191	93.25	18.94
10	182	100.50	15.93
11	133	107.00	15.07
12	132	113.00	19.99
13	131	118.75	21.69
14	103	123.00	23.97
15–16	124	128.50	17.26
17–18	119	133.50	17.60

Section 7:
Reliability

Reliability refers to how consistently any measurement estimates the characteristic in question, whether it be vocabulary, visual perception, intelligence, or self-confidence. In educational and psychological testing, reliability refers to how consistently, within the test itself, the items sample the domain of interest (internal consistency) or how consistently test results are produced over time (test-retest) or between different raters (interrater) (Salvia & Ysseldyke, 1991). According to Anastasi and Urbina (1997), coefficients at or above .80 are acceptable, while those of .90 and above are most desired; this is especially crucial when test results are the basis upon which important academic or remedial decisions may be made.

Internal Consistency

To assess the internal consistency, or homogeneity, of test items, Cronbach's coefficient alpha was computed at each age level. This statistic yields an estimate of the uniformity of the test items based on their intercorrelations. Another measure of internal consistency is the split-half coefficient, which in this case is the correlation between the scores derived from the odd-numbered items with scores from even-numbered items.

High correlations from each of these analyses indicate homogeneity of the test items and provide an index of the amount of error associated with the test results. Coefficient alpha and split-half reliability coefficients were computed by age group for all individuals participating in the standardization study. These coefficients, shown in Table 7.1, are relatively high for all age groups. Coefficient alphas range from .93 to .98 with a median of .96; split-half coefficients, corrected for the full length of the test, range from .96 to .99 with a median of .98.

TABLE 7.1
Internal Consistency Reliability Coefficients by Age Group

Age Group	Alpha	Split-Half	
		Uncorrected	Corrected
2	.93	.92	.96
3	.96	.95	.98
4	.96	.96	.98
5	.95	.92	.96
6	.96	.94	.97
7	.96	.93	.97
8	.95	.93	.96
9	.97	.96	.98
10	.96	.93	.97
11	.96	.95	.98
12	.97	.96	.98
13	.98	.96	.98
14	.98	.97	.99
15–16	.97	.95	.98
17–18	.97	.96	.98
Median	.96	.95	.98

Temporal Stability

Test-retest reliability provides evidence of the stability with which a test assesses the same individual over time. To examine the temporal stability of the EOWPVT, 226 examinees were each retested by the same examiner. The average duration between the first and second testing was 20 days.

Table 7.2 shows the demographic characteristics of this group, and Table 7.3 shows the correlations of standard scores obtained for five age groupings. Correlations were corrected for range based on the standard deviation of the first testing (Guilford, 1954). The corrected test-retest correlations range from .88 to .97 with a coefficient of .90 for the entire sample. The test-retest coefficients provide evidence that use of the EOWPVT is sufficiently stable over time, in terms of the relative ranking of individuals from one testing to the next. Gain scores are also presented in Table 7.3. These range from a standard score gain of 2.31 to 5.62 with an average standard score gain of 3.39 for the entire sample. Overall, the magnitude of the gain scores is reasonable and can be explained in terms of practice effects. The gain score is highest for the youngest students in this sample, which may indicate that there is a greater practice effect for young children.

Interrater Reliability

Interrater reliability refers to the consistency with which different examiners are able to obtain the same rating of an examinee's ability. For the

TABLE 7.2
Demographic Characteristics of the Test-Retest Sample (N=226)

Characteristics	N	Percentage
Region:		
Northeast	15	6.6
North Central	108	47.8
South	67	29.7
West	36	15.9
Race/Ethnicity:		
Asian	3	1.3
Black	60	26.5
Hispanic	11	4.9
White	145	64.2
Other	7	3.1
Gender:		
Female	126	55.8
Male	100	44.2
Parent Education Level:		
Grade 11 or less	16	7.1
High School	57	25.2
1–3 Years College	60	26.5
4+ Years College	93	41.2
Residence:		
Urban	176	77.9
Rural	50	22.1
Educational Classification:		
Regular Ed.	226	100.0

EOWPVT, interrater reliability was evaluated in three different ways in order to examine different potential sources of error.

Reliability of Scoring

This first analysis consisted of an evaluation of the consistency with which examiners are able to follow the scoring procedure after the test has been administered. To conduct this study, 30 protocols were randomly selected from the standardization sample, two from each of the 15 age levels. Each protocol had been administered by a different examiner. The protocols showed items marked right or wrong but did not show an indication of a basal, ceiling, or a final raw score. Four scorers were asked to follow the procedures presented in this manual to obtain raw scores for each of the 30 pro-

TABLE 7.3
Test-Retest Reliability Coefficients by Age Group

Age Group	N	Test-Retest Uncorrected	Test-Retest Corrected	Mean Testing 1	Standard Deviation	Gain
2–4	26	.85	.88	98.41	13.46	5.62
4–7	74	.92	.89	102.41	17.91	2.31
8–10	63	.92	.91	105.20	16.33	3.99
11–13	34	.87	.94	102.68	10.43	3.36
14–18	29	.97	.97	103.55	15.43	2.87
Total	226	.91	.90	102.91	15.72	3.39

tocols based entirely on the item right or wrong markings on the protocols. Two of the scorers were trained, experienced scorers of this test and two had reference only to the instructions presented in this manual. Results were then compared to computer scoring of the protocols.

The results of this analysis showed 100 percent agreement between all scorers. This finding suggests that the method of scoring and the scoring instructions are sufficiently clear so that scoring can be carried out consistently. Careful attention to the scoring instructions is critical to obtaining meaningful results, and users of this test are urged to study the instructions and examples in this manual before using the test.

Reliability of Response Evaluation

The purpose of this analysis was to evaluate the consistency with which an examiner is able to score an individual's response as right or wrong.

For this analysis, the same 30 protocols selected for the above study were used. Examiners had been requested to write down examinees' responses to each item and to score each item as right or wrong as they administered the test. For the purpose of this study, all markings indicating right and wrong answers were removed from a copy of the protocols. A trained examiner then reviewed item responses written on the protocols by the 30 original examiners. Based on the written responses, the trained examiner rescored each item. These item scores were then compared to the original item scores. A total of 2,508 responses were compared. This comparison showed 99.4 percent agreement in item scoring between the trained examiner and the 30 original examiners.

Reliability of Administration

For this analysis 20 examinees were tested by two different examiners in the same testing session. The purpose of this study was to examine whether the test could be administered in a consistent way by different examiners. This analysis is of particular importance since the administration procedures for this edition of the test permit the examiners to provide cues to examinees when their first response to an item meets one of the criteria spelled out in the administration instructions. Failure to follow these instructions could lead to different raw scores. This analysis differs from an analysis of test-retest reliability in that the duration of time between testings is minimal and examiners from one testing to the next are different.

The 20 examinees participating in this study resided in an urban setting in California. All were white, regular education students. Nine were females and 11 were males. Their ages ranged from 3-0 to 17-6 with a median age of 9-5. Four examiners participated. Each had previous experience in administering the test. The order in which testing 1 and testing 2 was assigned to each examiner was counterbalanced.

Following administration, the protocols were scored by a single examiner. Raw scores were converted to standard scores, and the correlation of testing 1 with testing 2 was obtained along with means and standard deviations for each testing. The correlation between the two testings, corrected for range based on the standard deviation of the first testing (Guilford, 1954), is .93 (uncorrected r=.95). This shows a high degree of correspondence between the testing of the same individuals by different examiners. The means and standard deviations for the two testings are—testing 1: mean=124.19, SD=17.77; testing 2: mean=127.51; SD=15.67; with an average gain score of 3.32.

These results, taken together with those described above, suggest that the EOWPVT has a high level of interrater reliability.

Summary of Reliability Studies

Consideration of the three types of reliability evidence provided in this section suggests that the EOWPVT provides a consistent measure that is relatively free of error. The test is comprised of content that has a high level of homogeneity, it provides consistent measurement from one testing to the next, and it can be administered and scored consistently by different examiners. This high level of reliability was observed across all ages for which the test is intended. Based on these findings, users of the EOWPVT can have a high degree of confidence in the test's results.

Errors of Measurement

Scores obtained from any test are a composite of a person's "true ability" and some amount of error. It is, therefore, important to have a way to estimate the amount of error inherent in any set of observed scores. The Standard Error of Measurement (SEM) provides an estimate of error and is derived from the reliability coefficient of a score. The SEM is calculated using the formula:

$$SEM = SD \sqrt{1 - r}$$

where *SD* is the standard deviation of the distribution (e.g., 15 for standard scores) and *r* is the reliability coefficient, in this case Chronbach's alpha.

The more reliable the test, the smaller is the SEM. Using the SEM, a confidence interval within which the true score is likely to be found can be calculated. The calculated confidence interval is based on a specified degree of confidence. Table 7.4 lists the SEMs for raw scores and standard scores for two levels of confidence for all age groups.

For the purpose of establishing confidence intervals when interpreting test results, standard score values, representative of the values shown in Table 7.4, have been included on the record form for easy reference.

TABLE 7.4

Standard Errors of Measurement and 90% and 95% Confidence Levels for Raw Scores and Standard Scores by Age Group

Age Group	Raw Scores			Standard Scores		
	SEM	Confidence Level 90%	95%	SEM	Confidence Level 90%	95%
2	2.66	±4.38	±5.21	3.97	±6.55	±7.78
3	2.80	±4.62	±5.49	3.00	±4.95	±5.88
4	3.01	±4.97	±5.91	3.00	±4.95	±5.88
5	3.28	±5.42	±6.44	3.35	±5.53	±6.57
6	3.01	±4.96	±5.89	3.00	±4.95	±5.88
7	3.16	±5.22	±6.20	3.00	±4.95	±5.88
8	3.30	±5.45	±6.47	3.35	±5.53	±6.57
9	3.28	±5.41	±6.43	2.60	±4.29	±5.09
10	3.19	±5.26	±6.24	3.00	±4.95	±5.88
11	3.01	±4.97	±5.91	3.00	±4.95	±5.88
12	3.46	±5.71	±6.79	2.60	±4.29	±5.09
13	3.07	±5.06	±6.01	2.12	±3.50	±4.16
14	3.39	±5.59	±6.64	2.12	±3.50	±4.16
15–16	2.99	±4.93	±5.86	2.60	±4.29	±5.09
17–18	3.05	±5.03	±5.97	2.60	±4.29	±5.09
Median	3.07	±5.06	±6.01	3.00	±4.95	±5.88

Difference Scores

Because the EOWPVT and the *Receptive One-Word Picture Vocabulary Test* (ROWPVT) were conormed, information is provided for identifying significant and meaningful differences in performance.

Differences between expressive and receptive vocabulary scores for any examinee can be interpreted in light of two comparisons: (1) the *statistical significance* of the score difference and (2) the *frequency* of individuals in the normative sample having shown that score difference. The statistical significance is related to the probability that the score difference is obtained solely due to variability associated with errors of measurement. This is based on the SEM for each test and is calculated with the following formula:

$$\text{Difference Score} = Z \sqrt{SEM_e^2 + SEM_r^2}$$

where Z is the normal curve value associated with a desired significance level and SEM_e and SEM_r are the standard errors of measurement for the EOWPVT and the ROWPVT.

The frequency of score differences tells how common or rare such score differences are in the general population and are useful for interpreting test results. These values are based on the obtained score differences from individuals in the norms group.

Difference scores required for statistical significance and the percentage of examinees obtaining various score differences are presented in Appendix D in Tables D.4 and D.5.

Section 8:
Validity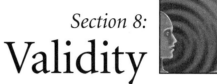

Validity is defined as the extent to which a test measures the construct it purports to measure (Anastasi & Urbina, 1997). The intent of test validation is to provide information that demonstrates whether appropriate and meaningful inferences can be made from a test (Messick, 1989). Three types of validity evidence are presented in this section: (1) *content validity*, which examines whether the test items adequately represent the particular domain for which the test was designed; (2) *criterion-related validity*, which examines how well the test's scores correlate with those from other tests known to assess the same ability; and (3) *construct validity*, which examines how well the test measures the ability or trait it is intended to measure.

Validity is a feature of a test that gains definition as evidence is accumulated. Test validation, therefore, is an ongoing process. Information about a test's validity provides evidence about the usefulness of a test for various purposes. This evidence serves to guide the user in evaluating the appropriateness of inferences made from the test.

Data presented in this section were obtained during the standardization study. Examiners were asked to provide results from several tests, with the requirement that the tests had been administered within one year of administration of the EOWPVT. For the purpose of direct comparison to the EOWPVT, all scores were converted to standard scores having a mean of 100 and a standard deviation of 15. The demographic characteristics of each group in the studies that follow are reported in Appendix C. Correlations, unless otherwise noted, were corrected for attenuation in the criterion and for range (Guilford, 1954).* All values, unless otherwise noted, are significant at or below the .05 level.

---

*The correction for attenuation is an adjustment to the correlation coefficient that accounts for errors of measurement in the criterion. The correction for range is an adjustment that yields a correlation coefficient that reflects the expected range of performance in the population, which for the EOWPVT is a distribution of standard scores with a standard deviation of 15.

Content Validity

Content validity is built into a test through its design specifications and through the procedures followed in item selection. Information relevant to content validity has been presented in the Development section of this manual and is summarized here.

For the EOWPVT, a format for the test was selected that would elicit single English words of progressive difficulty in response to the presentation of a series of illustrations. An important consideration in task design is whether or not the task taps other behaviors that might confound results. For example, a vocabulary test that requires the examinee to read a definition and then provide the word that matches the definition would yield results that could be confounded with reading ability. Because the task format of the EOWPVT requires the examinee only to view and name an illustration, the confounding effects of other skills is minimized.

Items were selected from a variety of sources to represent words that individuals at a given age level, regardless of their gender or cultural background, could be expected to have an equal likelihood of knowing. The easiest words on the test were obtained through parent questionnaires that asked parents to indicate the first words spoken by young children. The majority of the remaining words were selected with reference to their frequency of use in written material and the grade level at which the words appear in curriculum materials. Some relatively obscure words were also included to tap the highest levels of vocabulary ability. Only words that could be illustrated were selected.

Item analysis was the final step in item selection. The final items appearing on the EOWPVT were required to meet rigorous criteria of item discrimination and item bias studies. The final items were also selected to present difficulty levels appropriate for assessing a wide range of expressive vocabulary.

Criterion-Related Validity

Criterion-related validity shows how closely one set of scores is correlated with scores from other tests that directly and independently assess the same ability (Anastasi & Urbina, 1997). Concurrent validity is a type of criterion-related validity that is evaluated by correlating sets of scores from one test, such as the EOWPVT, with scores from another similar test taken by the same group at the same time or within a reasonably close time period. If the scores are highly correlated, it can be assumed that both tests tap the same skill.

Table 8.1 shows the correlations between the EOWPVT and several other vocabulary tests. The tests are listed as either expressive or receptive vocabulary tests. This identification is followed by a descriptor that identifies the task format of each test. The most prevalent format among the expressive tests listed below asks the examinee to provide a definition of a word either

TABLE 8.1
Correlations Between the EOWPVT and Tests of Vocabulary and Mean Standard Scores

Criterion Test	Criterion Format	N	Correlation Uncorrected	Correlation Corrected	Criterion Mean	Criterion SD	EOWPVT Mean	EOWPVT SD
EVT	Expressive Naming, Synonyms	26	.83	.72	87.27	25.79	86.77	20.02
PPVT-R	Receptive Picture I.D.	31	.62	.82	92.00	14.75	93.03	12.64
PPVT-III	Receptive Picture I.D.	67	.81	.76	88.00	19.90	86.97	17.38
ROWPVT	Receptive Picture I.D.	2,327	.75	.72	100.39	15.09	99.87	16.33
TOLD-P:3-PV	Receptive Picture I.D.	28	.57	.75	102.14	11.34	99.64	13.00
TOLD-P:3-RV	Expressive Category Naming		.68	.81	103.39	12.33		
TOLD-P:3–OV	Expressive Definitions		.67	.81	104.82	13.98		
WISC-III- Vocab.	Expressive Definitions	48	.78	.86	82.13	18.97	86.75	14.36
SB-4-Vocab.	Expressive Naming, Definitions	19	.64	.83	87.58	19.12	76.11	11.96
CAT5-Vocab.	Receptive Multi-task	41	.52	.68[a]	108.07	10.95	106.37	12.21
MAT7-Vocab.	Receptive Multi-task	23	.73	.90[a]	103.35	9.91	112.13	9.33
SAT9-Vocab.	Receptive Multi-task	53	.68	.67[a]	105.42	14.30	101.68	15.31

EVT: *Expressive Vocabulary Test* (Williams, 1997); PPVT-R: *Peabody Picture Vocabulary Test*-Revised (Dunn & Dunn, 1981); PPVT-III: *Peabody Picture Vocabulary Test-Third Edition* (Dunn & Dunn, 1997); ROWPVT: *Receptive One-Word Picture Vocabulary Test* (Brownell, 2000); TOLD-P:3: *Test of Language Development, Primary-Third Edition* (Newcomer & Hammill, 1997); PV: Picture Vocabulary, RV: Relational Vocabulary, OV: Oral Vocabulary; WISC-III: *Wechsler Intelligence Scale for Children-Third Edition* (Wechsler, 1991); SB-4: *Stanford-Binet Intelligence Scale-Fourth Edition* (Thorndike, Hagen & Sattler, 1986); CAT5: *California Achievement Test-Fifth Edition* (CTB/McGraw-Hill, 1992); MAT7: *Metropolitan Achievement Test-Seventh Edition* (Harcourt Brace Educational Measurement, 1992); SAT9: *Stanford Achievement Test-Ninth Edition* (Harcourt Brace Educational Measurement, 1996)

[a]Corrected for range only.

in synonym or sentence format. Two of the expressive tests include naming tasks similar to that of the EOWPVT, but this format represents only a portion of each of the tests. The majority of the receptive vocabulary tests ask the examinee to identify a picture from several alternatives that matches a word presented by the examiner. The multi-task vocabulary tests are group-administered, multiple-choice tests that include a variety of tasks that range from recognizing synonyms and antonyms to identifying the meaning of words in the context of a written passage.

The corrected correlations between the EOWPVT and these tests range from .67 to .90 with a median of .79. Correlations with tests of expressive vocabulary, overall, are not substantially higher than those with tests of receptive vocabulary (medians: expressive, .81; receptive, .76). Considering the wide range of dissimilarity of the task formats of these tests, the consistently strong correlations indicate that the EOWPVT is measuring the same behavior as the criterion tests. The difference in the task format of the EOWPVT accounts, in part, for the remaining variance between the tests.

Construct Validity

The evaluation of construct validity requires information from a variety of sources. Several assumptions underlie the use of the EOWPVT. Data is provided to address each of the following assumptions:

- **Chronological Age.** The extent of an individual's vocabulary increases as the individual matures; therefore, EOWPVT test scores should show a positive relationship to chronological age.
- **Cognitive Ability.** The relationship between vocabulary and cognitive ability is well documented; therefore, EOWPVT test scores should show a positive relationship to measures of cognitive ability.
- **Language.** Vocabulary is one aspect of the total complex of language skills, and these skills are interrelated; therefore, EOWPVT test scores should show a positive relationship to other language measures.
- **Academic Achievement.** Vocabulary and academic achievement are related; therefore, EOWPVT test scores should show a positive relationship to measures of academic achievement.
- **Expressive and Receptive Vocabulary.** Measures of expressive and receptive vocabulary, while related, tap unique processes. While a positive relationship should exist between EOWPVT test scores and measures of receptive vocabulary, unique variance should be present.
- **Previous Editions.** The current edition of the EOWPVT is expected to measure the same construct as previous editions of the test; therefore, a strong positive relationship should exist between the tests.
- **Exceptional Group Differences.** Because individuals who typically have academic difficulties are likely to show vocabulary deficits, EOWPVT test results should be lower for students having related disabilities.

Chronological Age

Evidence of the relationship of EOWPVT performance to chronological age is found in Table 6.5 in Section 6: Standardization. This table shows the smoothed raw score medians, which increase incrementally in relationship to the increasing age of individuals. This relationship can also be seen by the correlation of raw scores to chronological age. For the entire standardization sample, this correlation is .84 (uncorrected) and indicates that older individuals, who would be expected to have more well developed vocabularies, demonstrate greater proficiency on the EOWPVT.

Cognitive Ability

The strong relationship of vocabulary to cognitive ability is well documented (Bornstein & Haynes, 1998). With this expectation, correlations between the EOWPVT and measures of cognitive ability are of interest. Table 8.2 shows the correlation of the EOWPVT with the *Otis-Lennon School Ability Test–Seventh Edition* (OLSAT–7; Otis & Lennon, 1995). The OLSAT–7 measures abstract thinking and reasoning ability. The corrected correlation with the Verbal score is .88 and is .71 with the Nonverbal score. A multiple correlation of .89 between the EOWPVT and the two composite scores was obtained. Although the Verbal correlation is somewhat higher than that with the Nonverbal score, both correlations are relatively high, supporting the contention that EOWPVT performance is related to cognitive ability.

TABLE 8.2
Correlations Between the EOWPVT and Tests of Cognitive Ability and Mean Standard Scores

| Criterion Test | N | Correlation | | Criterion Test | | EOWPVT | |
		Uncorrected	Corrected	Mean	SD	Mean	SD
OLSAT-7							
Verbal	40	.74	.88[a]	105.15	12.27	110.78	10.39
Nonverbal		.39	.71[a]	110.28	12.21		
Verbal/Nonverbal		.78	.89[a]	—	—		

OLSAT-7: *Otis-Lennon School Ability Test-Seventh Edition* (Otis & Lennon, 1995)
[a]Corrected for range only.

Additional support for the relationship with cognitive ability comes from the exceptional groups data presented later in this section. If a relationship with cognitive ability exists, then individuals identified as having a low level of cognitive ability should perform significantly lower on the EOWPVT than individuals with average or above average ability. A comparison of the average performance of 51 individuals identified as mentally retarded to the mean of the norms group showed significantly lower performance by the mentally retarded group (*mean*=70.79, *SD*=11.39, *p*=.000).

Language

To examine the relationship of EOWPVT performance to other areas of language development, correlations with tests that provide relatively broad measures of language were calculated. The tests listed in Table 8.3 assess the individual's ability to comprehend and produce language. While skills at the word level are examined to some extent by these tests, the overriding focus of assessment is on language in connected discourse.

The corrected correlations in Table 8.3 show a strong relationship between performance on the EOWPVT and performance on these broader measures of language. The correlations range from .64 to .87 for subtest scores with a median of .75. Correlations with total scores range from .71 to .85 with a median of .76.

TABLE 8.3
Correlations Between the EOWPVT and Tests of Language and Mean Standard Scores

Criterion Test	N	Correlation Uncorrected	Corrected	Criterion Mean	SD	EOWPVT Mean	SD
CELF-3							
Expressive Language	50	.77	.87	91.88	18.77	91.74	12.57
Receptive Language		.75	.85	92.78	18.36		
Total Language		.75	.85	92.06	18.82		
OWLS							
Oral Expression	35	.81	.87	82.09	18.68	81.89	14.90
Listening Comprehension		.78	.85	83.37	17.31		
Oral Composite		.76	.80	82.63	16.94		
PLS-3							
Expressive Language	59	.55	.64	80.36	16.40	84.36	13.84
Auditory Comprehension		.67	.75	84.07	16.93		
Total Language		.63	.71	79.95	16.32		
TACL-R							
Word Classes & Relations	31	.57	.83	87.81	14.66	83.94	10.88
Grammatical Morphemes		.47	.75	83.65	17.17		
Elaborated Sentences		.36	.68	87.94	13.86		
Total		.43	.71	83.84	15.81		
TOLD-P:3							
Grammatic Understanding	28	.56	.75	98.75	14.18	99.64	13.00
Grammatic Completion		.63	.76	94.79	14.37		
Sentence Imitation		.56	.67	93.75	11.36		

CELF-3: *Clinical Evaluation of Language Functions-Third Edition* (Semel, Wiig & Secord, 1995); OWLS: *Oral and Written Language Scales* (Carrow-Woolfolk, 1995); PLS-3: *Preschool Language Scale-Third Edition* (Zimmerman, Steiner & Pond, 1992); TACL-R: *Test For Auditory Comprehension of Language-Revised* (Carrow-Woolfolk, 1985); TOLD-P:3: *Test of Language Development, Primary-Third Edition* (Newcomer & Hammill, 1997)

Academic Achievement

School achievement is related to a student's ability to extract information from what he or she hears and reads. Students with the most well developed vocabularies are able to understand a wider range of information with resulting increases in their educational attainment (Baker et al., 1998). If this is so, performance on tests of academic achievement should increase as a function of EOWPVT performance.

Correlations are shown to the Reading and Language composite scores of three widely used, group administered achievement tests. The Reading and Language composite scores of these tests survey a wide range of school-related skills. The Reading sections typically assess a range of vocabulary skills, such as word meanings, knowledge of synonyms and antonyms, multi-meaning words, and words in context as well as reading comprehension skills. The Language sections typically assess skills in usage and mechanics, such as grammar, spelling, and punctuation as well as study skills. The last test listed, the Reading subtest of the *Woodcock-Johnson Psychoeducational Battery–Revised* (WJ-R; Woodcock & Johnson, 1989), assesses basic skills in letter and word identification as well as passage comprehension.

Table 8.4 shows the relationship of EOWPVT performance to Reading and Language achievement. The corrected correlations with Reading achievement range from .61 to .85 with a median of .75. Those with Language achievement range from .58 to .86 with a median of .64. The magnitude of these correlations supports the hypothesis that a considerable relationship exists between performance on the EOWPVT and academic achievement in reading and language as measured by these tests.

Expressive and Receptive Vocabulary

The extent of an individual's vocabulary is the primary construct presumed to be measured by the EOWPVT and the ROWPVT. The tests differ, however, in that the EOWPVT is concerned with the individual's ability to use words; for the EOWPVT the stimulus is a visual representation of an object, action, or concept, and the response is a single word that describes that representation. The ROWPVT, in contrast, is concerned with the comprehension of words; for the ROWPVT the stimulus is a word and the response is the identification of an illustration that represents the word. EOWPVT performance requires word knowledge and the ability to access and retrieve a word from memory. ROWPVT performance requires word knowledge and does not have the added requirement of word retrieval.

The correlation between the standard scores for the standardization sample is .75 (uncorrected), which indicates a strong relationship between performance on the two tests. The square of the correlation coefficient provides an estimate of the shared variance between the tests. This calculation indicates that 56 percent of the variance in test performance between the two

TABLE 8.4

Correlations Between the EOWPVT and Tests of Academic Achievement and Mean Standard Scores

Criterion Test	N	Correlation		Criterion Test		EOWPVT	
		Uncorrected	Corrected	Mean	SD	Mean	SD
CAT5							
Reading	41	.41	.61[a]	107.73	9.40	106.37	12.21
Language		.46	.64[a]	109.27	10.92		
MAT7							
Reading	23	.56	.83[a]	108.70	9.38	112.13	9.33
Language		.63	.86[a]	109.52	9.97		
SAT9							
Reading	53	.71	.70[a]	105.23	15.69	101.68	15.31
Language		.60	.58[a]	106.17	13.32		
WJ–R							
Reading	21	.57	.85[a]	81.14	12.05	90.38	8.86

CAT5: *California Achievement Test-Fifth Edition* (CTB/McGraw-Hill, 1992); MAT7: *Metropolitan Achievement Test-Seventh Edition* (Harcourt Brace Educational Measurement, 1992); SAT9: *Stanford Achievement Test-Ninth Edition* (Harcourt Brace Educational Measurement, 1996); WJ-R: *Woodcock-Johnson Psychoeducational Battery-Revised* (Woodcock & Johnson, 1989)

[a]Corrected for range only.

tests can be accounted for by the same factor. The remaining 44 percent of the variance between the two tests is unique and due to other factors. Because of the differences in the stimulus-response modes of the two tests, the added requirement of word retrieval is likely to account for a substantial amount of this remaining variance.

Previous Editions

Although the current edition of the EOWPVT contains many items that did not appear on previous editions of the test, there is substantial item overlap. Since the construct on which these tests are based is the same, it is expected that there would be a strong relationship between performance on the current edition and past editions.

Table 8.5 shows that the corrected correlation between the current edition and the 1979 edition of the test is .86 and between the current edition and the 1990 edition is .85. These correlations are of a magnitude that is expected between parallel forms of a test.

Exceptional Group Differences

One of the purposes of the EOWPVT is to identify expressive vocabulary deficits in individuals who are having academic difficulties. It is expected

TABLE 8.5

Correlations Between the EOWPVT (2000 Edition) and Previous Editions and Mean Standard Scores

Criterion Test	N	Correlation		Criterion Test		EOWPVT	
		Uncorrected	Corrected	Mean	SD	Mean	SD
EOWPVT (1979)	67	.79	.86	96.22	15.28	90.25	13.45
EOWPVT–R (1990)	94	.82	.85	90.75	18.08	85.25	15.47

that individuals classified as having an academic-related disability would be more likely than the nonclassified population to show an expressive vocabulary deficit.

To explore this hypothesis, the EOWPVT standard scores of 1,023 examinees who had been identified as receiving special education or speech-language services were examined. Group membership was provided by the standardization study examiners who were asked to identify each examinee's disability status. When more than one disability was listed, the examinee was assigned to the group that represented the most severe disability. Eleven categories of exceptionality were identified. For each of the 11 groups, a t-test was conducted to identify significant differences between the average performance of each group and the estimate of the population mean, which is a standard score of 100.

Table 8.6 shows the mean standard score for each group and the probability associated with significance. The results are presented by group in order of greatest to least difference between the means. The mean differences of the first eight groups are significant. The composition of these groups reflects a wide range of disabilities typically associated with academic diffi-

TABLE 8.6
Comparison of the Standard Score Means of 11 Exceptional Groups to the Population Mean

Exceptionality	N	Mean	SD	Probability
Mentally Retarded	51	70.79	11.39	$p=.000$
Autistic	35	79.44	19.00	$p=.000$
Language Delay	208	81.15	13.86	$p=.000$
Exp./Rec. Lang. Disorder	141	84.40	16.52	$p=.000$
Behavioral Disorder	19	86.19	17.43	$p=.003$
Learning Disabled	143	87.62	14.39	$p=.000$
Hearing Loss	19	90.35	15.13	$p=.012$
Auditory Processing Deficit	28	92.05	13.02	$p=.003$
ADHD/ADD	21	97.38	16.33	$p=.470$ (ns)
Articulation	327	99.94	15.59	$p=.946$ (ns)
Fluency Disorder	31	100.05	15.00	$p=.985$ (ns)

culties. The ADHD/ADD group did not show significant differences. This is consistent with Purvis and Tannock's (1997) finding that children with ADHD/ADD did not have significantly impaired expressive and receptive language abilities. The articulation and fluency disorder groups, also, showed no significant differences in performance. This is as expected, since these are disorders of speech production rather than disorders of language usage or comprehension.

Conclusion

The data presented in this section lend strong support to the validity of the EOWPVT as an instrument for use in evaluating speaking vocabulary and for making related inferences. The validity of any instrument, however, must be continually reevaluated. Since the first edition of the EOWPVT, a number of research studies have been conducted. Because this information is relevant to the current edition, these studies are reviewed in the next section. To continue to add to the information concerned with the validity of this test, users of the EOWPVT are encouraged to submit studies pertaining to the validity of the test to the publisher.

Section 9:

Previous Research

Since the inception of the EOWPVT in 1979, many studies have compared the original and first revision of the test with other tests and have explored the use of the EOWPVT across diverse settings and populations. This section summarizes the research pertaining to criterion-related and construct validity. Although the current edition contains many new items, there is considerable item overlap with previous editions of the test. Data reported in the previous section show a strong statistical relationship between performance on the current edition and earlier editions. The studies reported in this section, therefore, provide an important source of additional information for evaluating the validity of the current edition of the EOWPVT.

Criterion-Related Validity

Previous studies of criterion-related validity examined the relationship of performance on earlier editions of the EOWPVT to that of other widely used, full-length vocabulary tests and vocabulary subtests of tests of cognitive ability or language. Table 9.1 summarizes this data. The following discussion provides a summary by type of test.

Several studies have compared performance on the previous editions of the EOWPVT to performance on full-length vocabulary tests. Correlations with the *Peabody Picture Vocabulary Test* (PPVT, Dunn, 1965; PPVT-R, Dunn & Dunn, 1981), which is a receptive vocabulary test, range from .58 to .80 with a median of .70. With the *Receptive One-Word Picture Vocabulary Test* (ROWPVT, Gardner, 1985a), also a test of receptive vocabulary, the correlation is .61. The correlation with the *British Picture Vocabulary Scale* (BPVS, Dunn et al., 1982) is .72. For the *Comprehensive Receptive and Expressive Vocabulary Test* (CREVT, Wallace & Hammill, 1994) the correlations with expressive vocabulary, which asks the examinee to name a synonym of the stimulus word, are .36 and .44 for the two forms of the test. For the receptive

TABLE 9.1
Criterion-Related Validity of Previous Editions of the EOWPVT

Correlations with the EOWPVT (1979)

Criterion Test	N	Ages	Disability	r	Source
BPVS	32	3–4	None	.72	Howlin & Cross, 1994
PPVT	215	2–3	None	Md, .70 (.67–.70)	Gardner, 1979
PPVT-R	36	4–5	None	.61	Channell & Peek, 1989
PPVT-R	66	6–10	LD	.80	Furlong & Teuber, 1984
PPVT-R	31	10–11	LD	.58	Furlong & Teuber, 1984
PPVT-R	32	3–4	None	.72	Howlin & Cross, 1994
PPVT-R	70	4	Lang. delay	.73	Kutsick et al, 1988
PPVT-R	42	na	Special ed.	.67	Wiesner & Beer, 1991
RLT Word Finding	28	8	Lang. delay	.74	Howlin & Kendall, 1991
TOLD-P Pic. Vocab.	36	4–5	None	.34	Channell & Peek, 1989
WISC-R Vocabulary	66	6–10	LD	.49	Furlong & Teuber, 1984
WISC-R Vocabulary	31	10–11	LD	.60	Furlong & Teuber, 1984
WPPSI Vocabulary	70	4	Lang. delay	.68	Kutsick et al, 1988

Correlations with the EOWPVT-R (1990)

Criterion Test	N	Ages	Disability	r	Source
DTLA–2 Word Opposites	436	6–11	None	.49	Gardner, 1990
CREVT					
Form A Exp.	27	na	Special ed.	.36	Wallace & Hammill, 1994
Form A Rec.				.77	
Form A General				.64	
Form B Exp.				.44	
Form B Rec.				.86	
Form B General				.78	
ROWPVT	59	8	None	.61	Gardner, 1990
PPVT–R	1,030	2–11	None	.59	Gardner, 1990
PVT	111	2–11	None	.76	Beery & Taheri, 1992
WISC–R Vocabulary	684	6–11	None	.47	Gardner, 1990
WPPSI–R Vocabulary	209	5–6	None	.48	Gardner, 1990

Correlations with the EOWPVT Upper Extension (1983)

Criterion Test	N	Ages	Disability	r	Source
PPVT–R	465	12–15	None	Md, .74 (.67–.70)	Gardner, 1983
WISC–R Vocabulary	465	12–15	None	Md, .83 (.74–.84)	Gardner, 1983

vocabulary subtest of the CREVT, the correlations are higher: .77 and .86. Correlations with the CREVT general vocabulary score, a composite of the two subtests, are .64 and .78 for Forms A and B. The correlation with the *Picture Vocabulary Test* (PVT, Beery & Taheri, 1992), which is an expressive vocabulary test similar in format to the EOWPVT, is .76.

With the vocabulary subtests of the *Wechsler Intelligence Test for Children* (WISC, Wechsler, 1949; WISC-R, Wechsler, 1974) and the *Wechsler Preschool and Primary Scale of Intelligence* (WPPSI, Wechsler, 1967; WPPSI-R, Wechsler, 1989), which require the examinee to provide a verbal definition of a word, the correlations range from .47 to .83 with a median of .64. The correlation with the word opposites subtest of the *Detroit Tests of Learning Aptitude-Second Edition* (DTLA-2, Hammill, 1985), is .49.

Correlations with vocabulary subtests of more comprehensive language tests are .34 for the *Test of Language Development–Primary* (TOLD-P, Hammill & Newcomer, 1982) picture vocabulary subtest and .74 for the *Renfew Language Tests* (RLT, Renfew, 1980) word finding vocabulary subtest.

Overall, correlations with other vocabulary tests range from .34 to .86 with a median of .67. This range of correlations is consistent with those reported for the current edition of the EOWPVT.

Construct Validity

For further evaluation of the construct validity of the EOWPVT, results from a number of studies are reported below. This research pertains to the relationship of EOWPVT performance to measures of cognitive ability, language, and academic achievement. Other studies concerned with differentiating groups are also summarized.

Cognitive Ability

The relationship of performance on previous editions of the EOWPVT to performance on tests of cognitive ability is summarized in Table 9.2. The results show a great deal of consistency in this relationship for groups of students having a range of disability status. Correlations with verbal composite scores are consistently higher than those for nonverbal performance scores. The correlations with the verbal portions of the tests account for the corresponding moderate to high correlations with full scale and total IQ scores. The correlations for the verbal scales range from .49 to .82 with a median of .57. Those with nonverbal performance scales, which include the *Columbia Mental Maturity Scale* (CMMS, Burgemeister, 1972) and the *Raven's Colored Progressive Matrices* (RCPM, Raven, 1985), range from .12 to .48 with a median of .38. Full scale and total IQ scores from the WPPSI, WPPSI-R, WISC-R, and *Stanford-Binet Intelligence Scales* (SBIS, Terman & Merrill, 1973) range from .61 to .78 with a median of .72. Similar results are reported for the multiple correlation of the PPVT-R and the EOWPVT with the WPPSI (Vance et al., 1989).

TABLE 9.2
**Summary of Studies of the Relationship of Cognitive Ability
to Previous Editions of the EOWPVT**

Correlations with the EOWPVT (1979)

Criterion Test	N	Ages	Disability	r	Source
CMMS	1,392	3–11	None	*Md,* .39 (.29–.59)	Gardner, 1979
RCPM	32	3–4	None	.37	Howlin & Cross, 1994
WISC-R					
VIQ	66	6–10	LD	.53	Furlong & Teuber, 1984
PIQ				.25	
WISC-R					
VIQ	31	10–11	LD	.49	Furlong & Teuber, 1984
PIQ				.12 (ns)	
WISC-R					
VIQ	42	na	Special ed.	.61	Wiesner & Beer, 1991
PIQ				.39	
Full Scale IQ				.61	
WPPSI					
Information	70	4	Lang. delay	.69	Kutsick et al 1988
Vocabulary				.68	
Arithmetic				.60	
Similarities				.76	
Comprehension				.65	
Animal House				.23	
Picture Completion				.52	
Mazes				.42	
Geometric Design				.27	
Block Design				.25	
VIQ				.82	
PIQ				.48	
Full Scale IQ				.78	
WPPSI					
VIQ	51	4	None	.89	Vance et al., 1989
PIQ				.60	Note: Correlations are multiple correlations of PPVT-R and EOWPVT
Full Scale IQ				.88	
SBIS IQ	32	3–6	Mild MR	.74	Goldstein et al., 1982

Correlations with the EOWPVT-R (1990)

Criterion Test	N	Ages	Disability	r	Source
WPPSI–R					
Information	93	4-5	None	.59	Gardner, 1990
Comprehension				.52	
Arithmetic				.36	
Vocabulary				.48	
Similarities				.42	
Full Scale IQ				.69	

Language

When EOWPVT scores were compared to those of tests that assess other aspects of language, moderate to high correlations were obtained. Correlations with the *Renfew Language Tests* (RLT, Action Picture Test, Renfew, 1980; The Bus Story, Renfew, 1981), the *Reynell Developmental Language Scales–Revised* (RDLS-R, Reynell, 1977), the *Test of Language Development–Intermediate* (TOLD-I, Hammill & Newcomer, 1982), and the *Test for Reception of Grammar* (TROG, Bishop, 1989) range from .51 to .84 with a median correlation of .73. These correlations, shown in Table 9.3, are consistent with the relationships reported between tests of language and the current edition of the EOWPVT.

TABLE 9.3
Summary of Studies of the Relationship of Language to Previous Editions of the EOWPVT
Correlations with the EOWPVT (1979)

Criterion Test	N	Ages	Disability	r	Source
RLT Action Picture					
Information	32	3–4	None	.84	Howlin & Cross, 1994
Grammar				.66	
RLT Action Picture					
Information	28	8	Lang. delay	.65	Howlin & Kendall, 1991
Grammar				.69	
RLT Bus Story					
Information	32	3–4	None	.51	Howlin & Cross, 1994
Sentence Length				.55	
RLT Bus Story					
Information	28	8	Lang. delay	.68	Howlin & Kendall, 1991
Sentence Length				.65	
RDLS-R					
Comprehension	32	3–4	None	.77	Howlin & Cross, 1994
RDLS-R					
Comprehension	28	8	Lang. delay	.73	Howlin & Kendall, 1991
Expression				.75	
TOLD-I	42	na	Special ed.	.75	Wiesner & Beer, 1991
TROG	32	3–4	None	.77	Howlin & Cross, 1994

Academic Achievement

Research concerned with the relationship of previous editions of the EOWPVT to academic achievement is summarized in Table 9.4. A correlation of .46 was obtained between the EOWPVT and the reading subtest of the *Test of Academic Achievement Skills* (TAAS, Gardner, 1989). Correlations with subtests of the *Test of Auditory-Perceptual Skills* (TAPS, Gardner, 1985b), which assesses auditory discrimination, memory, and comprehension, fall into the low to moderate range across subtests.

TABLE 9.4

Summary of Studies of the Relationship of Academic Achievement and Related Skills to Previous Editions of the EOWPVT

Correlations with the EOWPVT-R (1990)

Criterion Test	N	Ages	Disability	r	Source
TAAS					
Reading	22	8	None	.46	Gardner, 1990
TAPS					
Word Discrimination	58	4-5	None	.52	Gardner, 1990
Number Memory	64			.41	
Sentence Memory	62			.42	
Word Memory	63			.19 (ns)	
Interp. of Directions	62			.29	

Group Differences

Other studies have evaluated the performance of different groups of individuals to determine whether differences in mean scores would be obtained. Fifty normally developing Hispanic children in grades 3 to 5, bilingual in Spanish and English, were administered the EOWPVT (1979) (Teuber & Furlong, 1985). The students scored almost two standard deviations below the population mean. Mean performance for this group on the EOWPVT was a standard score of 74.6 (SD=18.7). Ruhl et al. (1992) examined the EOWPVT (1979) performance of 29 students identified as emotionally disturbed. The students ages ranged from 9 to 16. Comparison of the group mean to the population mean yielded significantly lower EOWPVT performance for this group. The mean standard score was 91.6 (t=3.02, df=28, p<.001).

To explore gender differences, Stoner and Spencer (1983) administered the EOWPVT (1979) to 52 female and 56 male Head Start students. The average age of the group was approximately 4 years. No significant differences in performance were obtained (t=.76, df=106, ns). The standard score mean for females was 92.38 (SD=13.69) and for males was 94.43 (SD=14.38). Wiesner and Beer (1991) also report no significant gender differences in EOWPVT (1979) performance for their sample of 15 females and 27 males ($F_{3,27}$=.40, ns). The mean standard score for females was 106.3 (SD=12.2) and for males was 109.9 (SD=17.1).

Conclusion

The findings of the research summarized in this section are consistent with that reported for the current edition of the EOWPVT. These findings indicate that the EOWPVT has a strong relationship to a wide range of measures of vocabulary and to the verbal portions of tests of cognitive ability. The relationship to other measures of language also tend to be strong, and correlations with language related measures of academic achievement are moderate.

References

Anastasi, A. & Urbina, S. (1997). *Psychological testing, 7th Edition*. Upper Saddle River, NJ: Prentiss-Hall, Inc.

Angoff, W. (1971). Scales, norms and equivalent scores. In R.L. Thorndike (Ed.), *Educational measurement, 2nd ed.* Washington: National Council on Education.

Au, T. (1986). A verb is worth a thousand words: The causes and consequences of interpersonal events implicit in language. *Journal of Memory and Language, 25,* 104-122.

Baker, S., Simmons, D., & Kameenui, E. (1998). Vocabulary acquisition: Research bases. In D. C. Simmons & E. J. Kameenui, Eds., *What reading tells us about children with diverse learning needs.* Mahwah, NJ: Lawrence Earlbaum Associates.

Baumann, J. F. & Kameenui, E. J. (1991). Research on vocabulary instruction: Ode to Voltaire. In J. Flood, J. J. D. Lapp & J. R. Squire, Eds., *Handbook of research on teaching the language arts.* New York, NY: Macmillan.

Becker, W. (1977). Teaching reading and language to the disadvantaged - what we have learned from field research. *Harvard Educational Review, 47,* 518-543.

Beery, K. E. & Taheri, C. M. (1992). *Beery Picture Vocabulary Test.* Odessa, FL: Psychological Assessment Resources.

Beitchman, J., Brownlie, E., Inglis, A. & Wild, J. (1994). Seven-year follow-up of speech/language impaired and control children: Speech/language stability and outcome. *Journal of the American Academy of Child & Adolescent Psychiatry, 33(9),* 1322-1330.

Beitchman, J. (Ed.), Cohen, N. (Ed.), Konstantareas, M. (Ed.), and Tannock, R. (Ed.). (1996). *Language, learning, and behavior disorders: Developmental, biological, and clinical perspectives.* New York, NY: Cambridge University Press.

Bishop, D. V. M. (1989). *Test for Reception of Grammar.* Cambridge, UK: D. Bishop.

Bishop, D., & Adams, C. (1990). A prospective study of the relationship between specific language impairment, phonological disorders and reading retardation. *Journal of Child Psychology and Psychiatry and Allied Disciplines, 31,* 1027-1050.

Bornstein, M. (1989). Stability in early mental development: From attention and information processing in infancy to language and cognition in childhood. In M. Bornstein & N. Krasnegor (Eds.), *Stability and continuity in mental development: Behavioral and biological perspectives.* Mahwah, NJ: Lawrence Erlbaum Associates.

Bornstein, M. & Haynes, O. (1998). Vocabulary competence in early childhood: Measurement, latent construct, and predictive validity. *Child Development, 69(3)* 654-671.

Bretherton, I., McNew, S., Snyder, L. & Bates, E. (1983). Individual differences at 20 months: Analytic and holistic strategies in language acquisition. *Journal of Child Language, 10,* 293-320.

Brownell, R. (2000). *Receptive One-Word Picture Vocabulary Test - Second Edition.* Novato, CA: Academic Therapy Publications.

Burgemeister, B. (1972). *Columbia Mental Maturity Scale, 3rd ed.* New York, NY: Harcort Brace Jovanovich.

Bus, A., Van Ijzendoorn, M. & Pellegrini, A. (1995). Joint book reading makes for success in learning to read: A meta-analysis on intergenerational transmission of literacy. *Review of Educational Research, 65,* 1-21.

Butler, S. R., Marsh, H. W., Sheppard, M.J. & Sheppard, J. L. (1985). Seven-year longitudinal study of the early prediction of reading achievement. *Journal of Educational Psychology, 77,* 349-361.

Carrow-Woolfolk, E. (1985). *Test for Auditory Comprehension of Language - Revised Edition.* Austin, TX: Pro-Ed.

Carrow-Woolfolk, E. (1995). *Oral and Written Language Scales.* Circle Pines, MN: American Guidance Service.

Channell, R. & Peek, M. (1989). Four measures of vocabulary ability compared in older preschool children. *Language, Speech & Hearing Services in Schools, 20(4),* 407-420.

Cole, N. & Moss, P. (1989). Bias in test use. In R.L. Linn (Ed.) *Educational Measurement, 3rd ed.* New York, NY: Macmillan.

Crocker, L. & Algina, J. (1986). *Introduction to classical and modern test theory.* New York, NY: Harcourt Brace Jovanovich College Publishers.

CTB/McGraw-Hill (1992). *California Achievement Tests, 5th ed.* Monterey, CA: CTB/McGraw-Hill.

Dale, E. & O'Rourke, J. (1981). *The Living Word Vocabulary.* Chicago, IL: World Book-Childcraft International, Inc.

DeMarco, S. & Bolen, L. (1990). Differential performance on the Expressive One Word Picture Vocabulary test. *Psychology in the Schools, 27(3),* 196-203.

Dunn, L. (1965). *Peabody Picture Vocabulary Test.* Circle Pines, MN: American Guidance Service.

Dunn, L. & Dunn, L. (1981). *Peabody Picture Vocabulary Test - Revised.* Circle Pines, MN: American Guidance Service.

Dunn, L. & Dunn, L. (1997). *Peabody Picture Vocabulary Test - Third Edition.* Circle Pines, MN: American Guidance Service.

Dunn, L., Dunn, L., Wheton, C., & Pintillie, D. (1982). *The British Picture Vocabulary Scale.* Windsor, UK: NFER-Nelson.

Fry, E. B., Fountoukidis, D. L., & Polk, J. K. (1993). *The New Reading Teacher's Book of Lists, 3rd Ed.* Englewood Cliffs, NJ: Prentice-Hall, Inc.

Furlong, M. & Teuber, J. (1984). Validity of the Expressive One Word Picture Vocabulary Test for learning-disabled children. *Journal of Psychoeducational Assessment, 2(1),* 29-36.

Gardner, M. (1979). *Expressive One-Word Picture Vocabulary Test.* Novato, CA: Academic Therapy Publications.

Gardner, M. (1983). *Expressive One-Word Picture Vocabulary Test - Upper Extension.* Novato, CA: Academic Therapy Publications.

Gardner, M. (1985a). *Receptive One-Word Picture Vocabulary Test.* Novato, CA: Academic Therapy Publications.

Gardner, M. (1985b). *Test of Auditory-Perceptual Skills.* Burlingame, CA: Psychological and Educational Publications.

Gardner, M. (1989). *Test of Academic Achievement Skills.* San Francisco, CA: Health Publishing Company.

Gardner, M. (1990). *Expressive One-Word Picture Vocabulary Test - Revised.* Novato, CA: Academic Therapy Publications.

Gerrig, R. & Banaji, M. (1994). Language and thought. In R. Sternberg (Ed.), *Thinking and problem solving. Handbook of perception and cognition, 2nd ed.* San Diego, CA: Academic Press.

Glaser, W. (1992). Picture naming. *Special Issue: Lexical access in speech production. Cognition, 42(1-3).* 61-105.

Goldstein, D., Allen, C. & Flemming, L. (1982). Relationship between the Expressive One-Word Picture Vocabulary Test and measures of intelligence, receptive vocabulary, and visual-motor coordination in borderline and mildly retarded children. *Psychology in the Schools, 19(3),* 315-318.

Guilford, J. P. (1954). *Psychometric Methods, 2nd ed.* New York, NY: McGraw-Hill.

Hambleton, R. K., Swaminathan, H., & Rogers, H. J. (1991). *Fundamentals of item response theory.* Newbury Park, CA: Sage Publications.

Hammill, D. (1985). *Detroit Tests of Learning Aptitude-2.* Austin, TX: Pro-Ed.

Hammill, D. & Newcomer, P. (1982). *The Test of Language Development - Primary.* Austin, TX: Pro-Ed.

Harcourt Brace Educational Measurement, (1992). *Metropolitan Achievement Test, 7th ed.,* San Antonio, TX: Harcourt Brace Educational Measurement.

Harcourt Brace Educational Measurement, (1996). *Stanford Achievement Test, 9th ed.,* San Antonio, TX: Harcourt Brace Educational Measurement.

Harris, A. J. & Jacobson, M. D. (1982). *Basic reading vocabularies.* New York, NY: Macmillan.

Henryssen, S. (1971). Gathering, analysing, and using data on test items. In R. L. Thorndike (Ed.), *Educational measurement, 2nd ed.* Washington, DC: American Council on Education.

Holland, P. W. & Thayer, D. T. (1988). Differential item performance and the Mantel-Haenszel procedure. In H. Wainer & H. I. Braum (Eds.), *Test Validity.* Mahwah, NJ: Lawrence Erlbaum Associates.

Howlin, P. & Cross, P. (1994). The variability of language test scores in 3- and 4-year old children of normal non-verbal intelligence: A brief research report. *European Journal of Disorders of Communication, 29(3),* 279-288.

Howlin, P. & Kendall, L. (1991). Assessing children with language tests: Which test to use? *British Journal of Disorders of Communication, 26(3),* 355-367.

Husband, T. H. & Hayden, D. C. (1996). Effects of the addition of color to assessment instruments. *Journal of Psychoeducational Assessment, 14,* 147-151.

Johnson, C. & Clark, J. (1988). Children's picture naming difficulty and errors: Effects of age of acquisition, uncertainty, and name generality. *Applied Psycholinguistics, 9(4),* 351-365.

Johnston, J. & Bowman, S. (1990). Gardner picture vocabulary tests: Relationship between performance in expression and reception. *International Journal of Clinical Neuropsychology, 12 (3-4),* 103-106.

Juel, C. (1988). Learning to read and write: A longitudinal study of 54 children from first through fourth grades. *Journal of Educational Psychology, 80,* 837-847.

Kucera, H. & Francis, W. N . (1967). *Computational analysis of present-day American English.* Providence, RI: Brown University Press.

Kutsick, K., Vance, B., Schwarting, F. & West, R. (1988). A comparison of three different measures of intelligence with preschool children identified at-risk. *Psychology in the Schools, 25(3),* 270-275.

Lim R. & Drasgow, F. (1990). Evaluation of two methods for estimating item response theory parameters when assessing differential item functioning. *Journal of Applied Psychology, 75 (2),* 164-174.

Linder, K. & Johnston, J. (1992) Grammatical morphology in language-impaired children acquiring English or German as their first language: A functional perspective. *Applied Psycholinguistics, 12(2),* 115-129.

Macnamara, J. (1982). *Names for things: A study of human learning.* Cambridge, MA: MIT Press.

Mandelbaum, D. (1949). *Selected writings of Edward Sapir in language, culture and personality. Selected essays.* Berkeley, CA: University of California Press.

Mann, V. (1984). Review: Reading skill and language skill. *Developmental Review, 4(1),* 1-15.

Mason, J. (1992). Reading stories to preliterate children: A proposed connection to reading. In P.B. Gough, L.C. Ehri & R. Treiman (Eds.), *Reading acquisition.* Mahwah, NJ: Lawrence Erlbaum Associates.

McDonald, J. (1997). Language acquisition: The acquisition of linguistic structure in normal and special populations. *Annual Review of Psychology, 48,* 215-41.

Merriam-Webster's Collegiate Dictionary (10th ed.). (1996). Springfield, MA: Merriam-Webster.

Messick, S. (1989). Validity. In R. L. Linn, ed., *Educational measurement, 3rd ed.* New York, NY: Macmillan.

Nagy, W. E. (1988). *Teaching vocabulary to improve reading comprehension.* Newark, DE: International Reading Association.

Nandakumar, R., Guttling, J. & Oakland, T. (1993). Mantel-Haenszel methodology for detecting item bias: An introduction and example using the guide to the assessment of test session behavior. *Journal of Psychoeducational Assessment, 11,* 108-119.

Newcomer, P. & Hammill, D. (1982). *Test of Language Development - Primary: Third Edition.* Austin, TX: Pro-Ed.

Newcomer, P. & Hammill, D. (1997). *Test of Language Development - Primary.* Austin, TX: Pro-Ed.

Otis, A. & Lennon, R. (1982). *Otis-Lennon School Ability Test.* San Antonio, TX: Harcourt & Brace.

Otis, A. & Lennon, R. (1995). *Otis-Lennon School Ability Test, 7th ed.* San Antonio, TX: Harcourt & Brace.

Pena, E., Quinn, R. & Iglesias, A. (1992). The application of dynamic methods to language assessment: A nonbiased procedure. *Journal of Special Education, 26(3),* 269-280.

Purvis, K. & Tannock, R. (1997). Language abilities in children with attention deficit hyperactivity disorder, reading disabilities, and normal controls. *Journal of Abnormal Child Psychology, 25(2),* 133-144.

Rapin, I. (1996). Practitioner review: Developmental language disorders: A clinical update. *Journal of Child Psychology and Psychiatry, 37 (6),* 643-655.

Raven, J. C., Court, J. H., & Raven, J. (1985). *A manual for Raven's Progressive Matrices.* London, UK: H. K. Lewis.

Renfrew, C. E. (1981) *The Bus Story.* Oxford, UK: C. E. Renfrew.

Renfrew, C. E. (1980) *The Renfrew Language Tests.* Oxford, UK: C. E. Renfrew.

Renfrew, C. E. (1989). *Action Picture Test, 3rd ed.* Oxford, UK: C. E. Renfrew.

Reynell, J. (1977). *Reynell Developmental Language Scales - Revised.* Windsor, UK: NFER-Nelson.

Rice, M. (1983). Contemporary accounts of the cognition/language relationship: Implications for speech-language clinicians. *Journal of Speech and Hearing Disorders, 48(4),* 347-359.

Rice, M. & Kemper, S. (1984). *Child language and cognition.* Baltimore, MD: University Park Press.

Rose, S., Feldman, J., Wallace, I. & Cohen, P. (1991). Language: A partial link between infant attention and later intelligence. *Developmental Psychology, 27(5),* 798-805.

Ruhl, K. L., Hughes, C. A. & Camarata, S. M. (1992). Analysis of the expressive and receptive language characteristics of emotionally handicapped students served in public school settings. *Journal of Childhood Communication Disorders, 14 (2),* 165-176.

Salvia, J. & Ysseldyke, J. W. (1991). *Assessment, 5th ed.* Boston: Houghton-Mifflin.

Scarr, S. & McCartney, K. (1988). Far from home: An experimental evaluation of the Mother-Child Home Program in Bermuda. *Child Development, 59,* 531-543.

Semel, E., Wiig, E. & Secord, W. (1995). *Clinical Evaluation of Language Fundamentals, 3rd ed.* San Antonio, TX: The Psychological Corporation.

Simmons, D. & Kameenui, E. (1990). The effect of task alternatives on vocabulary knowledge: A comparison of students with learning disabilities and students of normal achievement. *Journal of Learning Disabilities, 23(5),* 291-297.

Stahl, S. A. (1999). *Vocabulary Development.* Cambridge, MA: Brookline Books.

Stanovich, K. (1986). Matthew effects in reading: Some consequences of individual differences in the acquisition of literacy. *Reading Research Quarterly, 21,* 360-406.

Stanovich, K. (1988). Explaining the differences between the dyslexic and the garden variety poor reader: The phonological—core variable—difference model. *Journal of Learning Disabilities, 21,* 590-604.

Stoner, S. & Spencer, W. (1983). Sex differences in expressive vocabulary of Head Start children. *Perceptual & Motor Skills, 56(3),* 1008.

Swaminathan, H. & Rogers, J. (1990). Detecting differential item functioning using logistic regression procedures. *Journal of Educational Measurement, 27(4),* 361- 370.

Swanson, H. L. (1986). Do semantic memory deficiencies underlie learning readers' encoding processes? *Journal of Experimental Child Psychology, 41,* 461-488.

Taylor, S. E., Frackenpohl, H., White, C. E., Nierroda, B. W., Browning, C. L. & Birsner, E. (1989). *EDL core vocabularies in reading, mathematics, science, and social studies.* Columbia, SC: Educational Development Laboratories.

Terman, L. M. (1916). *The measurement of intelligence.* Boston, MA: Houghton-Mifflin.

Terman, L. M. & Merrill, M. A. (1973). *Stanford-Binet Intelligence Scale.* Boston, MA: Houghton-Mifflin.

Teuber, J. & Furlong, M. (1985). The concurrent validity of the Expressive One Word Picture Vocabulary Test for Mexican-American children. *Psychology in the Schools, 22(3),* 269-273.

Thorndike, R., Hagen, E. & Sattler, J. (1986). *Stanford-Binet Intelligence Scale, 4th ed.* Itasca, Il: Riverside Publishing.

U.S. Bureau of the Census. (1998). *Statistical Abstract of the United States.* Washington, DC: U.S. Department of Commerce.

U.S. Department of Education. (1995). *Seventeenth annual report to Congress on the implementation of the individuals with disabilities act.* Washington, DC: U. S. Government Printing Office.

Vance, B., West, R. & Kutsick, K. (1989). Prediction of Wechsler Preschool and Primary Scale of Intelligence IQ scores for preschool children using the Peabody Picture Vocabulary Test-R and the Expressive One Word Picture Vocabulary Test. *Journal of Clinical Psychology, 45(4),* 642-644.

Wallace, G. & Hammill, D. (1994). *Comprehensive Receptive and Expressive Vocabulary Test.* Austin, TX: Pro-Ed.

Warren, S. & Yoder, P. (1997). Communication, language and mental retardation. In MacLean, W. (Ed.), *Ellis' handbook of mental deficiency, psychological theory and research, 3rd ed.* Mahwah, NJ: Lawrence Erlbaum Associates.

Wechsler, D. (1949). *Manual for the Wechsler Intelligence Scale for Children.* New York: The Psychological Corporation.

Wechsler, D. (1967). *Manual for the Wechsler Preschool and Primary Scale of Intelligence.* New York: The Psychological Corporation.

Wechsler, D. (1991). *Wechsler Intelligence Scale for Children - 3rd ed.* San Antonio, TX: The Psychological Corporation.

Wechsler, D. (1974). *Wechsler Intelligence Scale for Children - Revised.* New York, NY: The Psychological Corporation.

Wechsler, D. (1989). *WPPSI-R Manual: Wechsler Preschool and Primary Scales of Intelligence - Revised.* San Antonio, TX: Psychological Corporation.

Whitehurst, G. (1996). Language processes in context: Language learning in children reared in poverty. In L.B. Adamson & M. A. Romski, eds., *Research on communication and language disorders: Contribution to theories of language development.* Baltimore, MD: Brookes.

Whitehurst, G. & Lonigan, C. (1998). Child development and emergent literacy. *Child Development, 69 (3),* 848-872

Wiesner, M. & Beer, J. (1991). Correlations among WISC-R IQs and several measures of receptive and expressive language for children referred for special education. *Psychological Reports, 69 (3, pt 1),* 1009-1010.

Williams, K. (1997). *Expressive Vocabulary Test.* Circle Pines, MN: American Guidance Service.

Woodcock, R. W. & Johnson, M. B. (1989). *Woodcock-Johnson Psycho-Educational Battery - Revised.* Itasca, IL: Riverside Publishing.

Zeno, S. M., Ivens, S. H., Millard, R. T. & Duvveri, R. (1995). *The educator's word frequency guide.* Brewster, NY: Touchstone Applied Science Associates, Inc.

Zimmerman, I., Steiner, V. & Pond, R. (1992). *Preschool Language Scale - 3.* San Antonio, TX: The Psychological Corporation.

APPENDIX A
Examples of Incorrect and Cued Responses

Examples listed in this appendix represent either the most frequently obtained incorrect responses or typical incorrect responses. Examples of cued responses are not exhaustive, and other responses are expected that will require a cue from the examiner.

Item	Incorrect Response	Cued Response
1. boat	car	
2. tree	bush	
3. apple	pear	
4. eye(s)	ears	
5. kitty/ kitten/ cat	dog	pet/ "What kind?"
6. (tele)phone	radio	
7. bird	squirrel	sparrow/ "What else is this called?"
8. scissor(s)	cut	
9. bus	train, car, truck	
10. swing	slide	
11. bike/ bicycle	motorcycle, bus, car	
12. sofa/ couch	chair	
13. plane/ airplane/ jet	helicopter	
14. book	box	
15. duck	turkey, chicken, goose	bird/ "What kind?"
16. train	truck, bus	
17. leaf	tree, flag	
18. watch	clock, timer	
19. truck	car, bus, van	
20. computer	TV	
21. corn	carrot	
22. paint(er/ing)	washing	man/ "What's he doing?"
23. kite	flag, fly	
24. wagon	pull, toy	
25. chicken/ hen/ rooster	turkey, duck	bird/ "What kind?"
26. cup	drink, bowl	
27. basket	bowl, bag	
28. ear	hat	head/ (point to arrow) "What's this?"
29. wheel	tire, bike	spokes/ (circle illustration) "What's this?"
30. cloud(s)	smoke	sky/(point to arrow) "What's this?"
31. tiger	lion	
32. smoke	clouds	chimney/ (point to arrow) "What's this?"
33. mermaid	girl, fairy	
34. animal(s)	(various)	(names items)/ (circle illustration) "What word names all of these?"
35. wall	bed	window, curtains/ (point to arrow) "What's this?"
36. penguin	seal, duck	bird/ "What kind?"
37. bug(s)/insect(s)	animals	(names items)/ (circle illustration) "What word names all of these?"
38. starfish/sea star	octopus, seashell	
39. clothes	(various)	(names items)/ (circle illustration) "What word names all of these?"
40. tire	wheel	
41. bridge	building, train track, gate	road/ (point to bridge) "What's this?"
42. suitcase(s)/luggage/ baggage/bag(s)	baskets, boxes, briefcases, packages, vacation	(names items)/ (circle illustration) "What word names all of these?"
43. skateboard	skate, rollerblade	

Item	Incorrect Response	Cued Response
44. footprint(s)	feet, feetprints, footsteps, foot marks	
45. fruit	vegetables	food/ "What kind?"
46. skeleton	bones, body, man	
47. light(s)	night	(names items)/ (circle illustration) "What word names all of these?"
48. (fish) tank/ aquarium	box, cage, goldfish	
49. raccoon	squirrel, fox, skunk	animal/ "What kind?"
50. food	dinner, lunch	(names items)/ (circle illustration) "What word names all of these?"
51. antler(s)/ horn(s)	ears	reindeer, deer/ (point to arrow) "What's this?"
52. sew(ing)	knitting, cutting	man/ "What's he doing?"
53. drink(s)/ beverage(s)/ refreshment(s)	cups, snack	(names items)/ (circle illustration) "What word names all of these?"
54. fireplace	chimney, fire, smoke	bricks/ (circle illustration) "What's this?"
55. dentist	nurse, teeth	doctor/ "What kind?"
56. furniture	bedroom, seats, house stuff	(names items)/ (circle illustration) "What word names all of these?"
57. cactus	tree, dangerous	desert/ (point to cactus) "What's this?"
58. statue(s)	trophies, stone	
59. binocular(s)	camera, glasses, goggles	
60. wrench	screwdriver, pliers	tool/ "What kind?"
61. instrument(s)	music, toys, band	(names items)/ (circle illustration) "What word names all of these?"
62. pineapple	pinecone, porcupine	fruit/ "What kind?"
63. stool	bench, chair	seat/ "What kind?"
64. fly(ing)/ flight	air, sky, wings	(names items)/ (circle illustration) "What word names all of these?"
65. telescope	microscope, binoculars	scope/ "What kind?"
66. goat	sheep, lamb, deer	animal/ "What kind?"
67. mail	letters, envelopes	
68. ostrich	peacock, turkey, flamingo	bird/ "What kind?"
69. rectangle/ parallelogram	square, triangle, block, box	shape/ "What kind?"
70. leopard/ jaguar/ cheetah	tiger, lion	animal/ "What kind?"
71. compass	clock, watch	
72. shield	badge, armor	
73. write(ing)/ draw(ing)	supplies, pencils	(names items)/ (circle illustration) "What word names all of these?"
74. lobster/ crawfish/ crawdad	crab, shrimp, scorpion, bug	
75. thermometer	temperature, measuring	
76. America/ U.S.(A.)/ United States (of Amer.)	Earth, Africa, world	map/ "What kind?"
77. saddle	horse seat, cowboy thing	
78. trumpet	flute, trombone, music	instrument, horn/ "What kind?"
79. wheelbarrow	wagon, barrel	
80. percent	division, price	math sign/ "What kind?"
81. windmill	fan, satellite, weathervane	
82. paw	foot, claw	
83. chess	checkers, chest	game/ "What kind?"
84. tweezer(s)	clippers, pinchers, pliers	

Examples of Incorrect and Cued Responses

Item	Incorrect Response	Cued Response
85. time	clocks, watches	(names items)/ (circle illustration) "What word names all of these?"
86. stadium/ arena	baseball, ball game	
87. stump	trunk, tree, log	
88. cut(ting)/ sharp	knives, working	tools/ "What kind?"
89. pyramid(s)	tents, triangles, mountains	
90. skydive(er(s)/ing)/ parachute(er(s)/ing)	flying, astronaut	jumping/ "What else is this called?"
91. measure(ers/ing)	temperature	(names items)/ (circle illustration) "What word names all of these?"
92. reptile(s)	mammals, amphibians	animals/ "What kind?"
93. celery	broccoli, cabbage, lettuce	vegetable/ "What kind?"
94. transportation/ travel/ vehicle(s)	driving, engines, move	(names items)/ (circle illustration) "What word names all of these?"
95. spring(s)	spirals, coils, wires	
96. banjo	guitar, violin, ukulele	instrument/ "What kind?"
97. graph/ chart	map, grid, degrees, scale	
98. boomerang	frisbee, sling shot, sock	toy/ "What kind?"
99. greenhouse	garden, barn, shed	
100. dock/ pier	bridge, deck, boardwalk	water, lake/ (point to dock) "What's this?"
101. hoof	paw	foot/ "What kind?"
102. water	letters, oxygen, H2O	chemical/ "What kind?"
103. direction(s)	signs, travel, arrows	(names items)/ (circle illustration) "What word names all of these?"
104. microscope	telescope, magnifier	scope/ "What kind?"
105. hammock	swing, cot, lounge, relax	
106. Africa	South America, state	map, continent/ "What kind?"
107. feeling(s)/ emotion(s)/ reaction(s)/ expression(s)	faces, people, actions, children	(names emotions)/ (circle illustration) "What word names all of these?"
108. seasoning(s)/ spice(s)	salts, shakers, cans, jars	
109. funnel	horn, filter, tube	
110. battery	sink, motor, radio	
111. scroll	map, script, paper, letter	Torah/ "What else is this called?"
112. clarinet	flute, oboe, horn	instrument/ "What kind?"
113. scale(s)/ balance	weigher	
114. bulldozer	tractor, plow, construction	vehicle/ "What kind?"
115. appliance(s)	utilities, cooking, electricity	
116. hexagon	octagon, pentagon, stop sign	shape/ "What kind?"
117. column/ pillar	pole, stand, statue	
118. reel	cast, motor, wheel	fishing rod/ (point to arrow) "What's this?"
119. stethoscope	telescope, Dr. thing, heart	
120. hourglass	time, clock	timer/ "What kind?"
121. hurdle(er/ing)	gymnastics, jumping, track	
122. monument(s)/ memorial(s)	statues, buildings	(names items)/ (circle illustration) "What word names all of these?"
123. anvil	anchor, iron	
124. otter	beaver, seal, weasel	animal/ "What kind?"
125. kayak	canoe, raft	boat/ "What kind?"
126. clamp	screw, vise	tool/ "What kind?"
127. rodent(s)	furry, wild, reptiles	animals, mammals/ "What kind?"
128. communication/ information	entertainment, electronics, media, news	(names items)/ (circle illustration) "What word names all of these?"

Item	Incorrect Response	Cued Response
129. symbol(s)/ sign(s)	medicine, health, directions	
130. beret	painting hat, French hat	hat, cap/ "What kind?"
131. sphinx	Egyptian, pyramid	statue/ "What kind?"
132. fungus(i/es)	mushrooms	(names items)/ (circle illustration) "What word names all of these?"
133. tripod	telescope, camera, surveyor	stand/ "What kind?"
134. percussion	music, band	instruments/ "What kind?"
135. protractor	compass, ruler, scale	tool/ "What kind?"
136. stirrup	saddle, foot holder	
137. hieroglyphic(s)	Egyptian, shapes	symbols/ "What kind?"
138. clef(s)	music, notes	(names items)/ (circle illustration) "What word names all of these?"
139. rhomboid/ parallelogram	quadrilateral, rectangle, rhombus, trapezoid	shape/ "What kind?"
140. squeegee	scraper, paint brush	
141. thermostat	heater, temperature	
142. beaker	measuring cup	measurer/ "What kind?"
143. poultry/ fowl	feathers, food	birds, animals/ "What kind?"
144. yoke	horse shoe, holster, noose	
145. observatory	laboratory, dome, lighthouse, planetarium	telescope/ (circle illustration) "What's this?"
146. prescription	poison, health, drug store	
147. tine/ prong	finger, tong	fork/ (point to arrow) "What's this?"
148. metronome	scale, clock, pendulum	
149. abacus	math, toy	counter/ "What kind?"
150. silhouette	shadow, ink blot, detective	
151. filament	coil, wire, spring	light bulb/ (point to arrow) "What's this?"
152. thistle	flower, dandelion, thorn	plant, weed/ "What kind?"
153. gauge(s)/ meter(s)	radios, electricity, heaters	
154. survey(or/ing)	engineer, looking, telescope	
155. candelabra	lamp	candlestick holder/ "What kind?"
156. sickle	hook, reaper, slingblade	
157. pommel/ horn	holster, handle	saddle/ (point to arrow) "What's this?"
158. invertebrate(s)	insects, herbivores	
159. tangent	ball, loop, circle, slope	
160. monocular	binocular, camera, telescope	
161. scarab	beetle, fossil, bug	
162. sphere	globe, circle, circumference	
163. trowel	smoother, spreader, iron	
164. shard	artifacts, clay	pottery/ (point to arrow) "What's this?"
165. sextant	compass, pendulum, arc	
166. caster	wheel	
167. outrigger	canoe, catamaran	boat/ "What kind?"
168. louver	blinds, shutters, slats	door/ (point to arrow) "What's this?"
169. plinth	base, pedestal, stand	column, pillar/ (point to arrow) "What's this?"
170. dolmen	rock, table, altar	

APPENDIX B
Participants and Test Sites

This appendix lists individuals who participated in the development of this edition of the EOWPVT as well as test sites. Only those participants who gave their permission to be listed are included.

Cultural Review Panel

Rose M. Alvarado, BA
Speech & Language Specialist
Alisal Teacher's Association
Salinas, CA

Debra Causey, MS
Speech & Language Pathologist
Baldwin County Schools
Milledgeville, GA

Charles G. Go, PhD
Youth Development Advisor
University of California Cooperatve
Extension
Alameda, CA

Bette Goldstein, MSEd, LDTC
Resource Room Director
Magen David Yeshivah
Brooklyn, NY

Johnna L. Wingate, BS
Speech Language Pathologist
Children's Care Hospital and School
Outreach
Rapid City, SD

Consultants

Claudia Chittenden, MA, CCC-SLP
Marin County Office of Education
San Rafael, CA

Jerry Stemach, MS, CCC-SLP
Sonoma County Office of Education
Sonoma, CA

Tracy Totman, MA, CCC-SLP
Marin County Office of Education
San Rafael, CA

Gail P. Venable, MS, CCC-SLP
Speech Language Pathologist
San Francisco, CA

Examiners

NORTHEAST
CONNECTICUT
Orange
Susan R. Bozso, MSEd, CFY-SLP
Nancy A. Gargano, MS, CCC-SLP
Denise M. McLinden, MS, CCC-SLP
Sharon L. Offney, MS, CCC-SLP
Stamford
Robin Story, PhD, CCC-SLP
MASSACHUSETTS
Boston
Clinical Supervisory Staff, CCC-SLP, Robbins Speech, Language & Hearing Center at Emerson College
New Bedford
Cheryl Bernier, MS, CCC-SLP
Donna Karalekas, BA
Rosalind Leahey, MEd, SLP
Diane Leclair, MS, CAGS, SLP
Diane M. Metthe, MA, SLP
Olinda Morrison, BA
Ana Raposo, BA
NEW HAMPSHIRE
Manchester
Susan O'Connor, MEd, CCC-SLP
NEW JERSEY
Howell
Patricia E. Kossoy, MA, CCC-SLP
Katherine Papazoglou, MA, CCC-SLP
Milltown
Doretta C. Helfgott, BA
NEW YORK
Albertson
Alice Azzara, MA, CCC-SLP
Celeste McDonald, MA, CCC-SLP
Alexander
Susan Privitera, MS, SLP
Amherst
Linda Bosshardt, MS, CCC-SLP
Alicia Campbell, MA, CCC-SLP
Camela Ludwick, MA, CCC-SLP
Brooklyn
Bette Goldstein, MA, LDTC

Buffalo
Holly Tedesco, MA, SLP
Oceanside
Emily Weinstein, MS, CCC-SLP
Poughkeepsie
Karyn Quan Joyce, MS, CCC-SLP
Lisa Struss, MS, CCC-SLP
Red Hook
Kelly LaFalce, MA, CCC-SLP
Rifton
Jennifer A. Petruski, MS, CCC-SLP
Sayville
Robin P. Solomon, MSEd, TSHH
Sherman
Cynthia Gabriel, MA, CCC-SLP
PENNSYLVANIA
Franklin
Heather A. Buchanan, MA, CCC-SLP
New Oxford
Grace Azzara
Joe Azzara
Perryopolis
Karen Mimnaugh, MA

NORTH CENTRAL
ILLINOIS
Chicago
Mary Hollis Johnston, PhD
East Moline
Jean Petsche, MA, CCC-SLP
Annette Teslik, MS, CCC-SLP
Fulton
Kimberly Klooster, MS, CCC-SLP
Lexington
Tara Anderson, MS, SLP
Normal
Kristyn J. Ricketts, MS, CCC-SLP/L
Norridge
Judith M. Dreyer, BS
Oakbrook Terrace
Leona M. Hubatch, PhD, CCC
Janet L. Weberling, MA, CCC
Pleasant Plains
Diane K. Covey, MA, CCC-SLP
Pontiac
Mary A. Billington, MS, CCC-SLP/L
Kristin McIlrath, MA, CCC-SLP/L

Peggy Modglin, MS, CCC-SLP/L
Skokie
Karen L. Diaz, MS, CCC-SLP
INDIANA
East Chicago
Meridy Jackson, MS, SLP
Karen A. Lebryk, MS, SLP
Kathryn Nagdemann, MA, CCC-SLP
Carol Peterson, MA
Evansville
J. Lynette Fredrickson, MS, CCC-SLP
Kelli A. Lumaye, MA, CF/SLP
Janet Mabis, MS, CCC-SLP
Cindy K. McWilliams, MS, CCC-SLP
Lisa Nally, MA, CCC-SLP
Mary Melissa Robison, MS, CCC-SLP
KANSAS
Kansas City
Jenny R. Helzer, MA, CCC-SLP
Julie A. Prevost, MA, CCC-SLP
Kerri Tuttle Schreiber, MA, CCC-SLP
Wichita
Julie M. Foster, MA, CCC-SLP
Judy C. Johnson, MA, CCC-SLP
Karen Kuhn, MA, CCC-SLP
Donna J. Reid, MA, CCC-SLP
Daneen J. Stahl, BA, CDSO
Deborah Tremain, MA, CCC-SLP
Rebecca L. Werner, MA, CCC-SLP
Stacey Windholz, MA, CCC-SLP
MICHIGAN
Clinton
Gail Kennedy Elliott, MA, CCC-SLP
Hillsdale
Daniel A. Hanks, MA, CCC-SLP
Muskegon
Millicent Smits, MA, CCC-SLP
Ravenna
Julie A. Raynor, MA, CCC-SLP
OHIO
Bedford
Judy Walsh, MA, CCC-SLP
Fairview Park
Mary Z. Barnes, MA, CCC-SLP
SOUTH DAKOTA
Lennox
David J. Schieffer, MA

Rapid City
Johnna L. Wingate, BS
WISCONSIN
Markesan
Marian Krueger, BS
Milwaukee
Jane Ashpes, MS, CCC-SLP
Joanne R. Bischoff, MS, CCC-SLP
Anne-Guri E. Bishop, MS, CCC-SLP
Ruth Brook, MS, CCC-SLP
Judith Clark, MS, CCC-SLP
Wendy Heuser Dettman, MS, CCC-SLP
Mary M. Gantz, MS, CCC-SLP
Ellie Graan, MS, CCC-SLP
Sue Gruenwald, MS, CCC-SLP
M. Siobhan Haggerty, MS, CCC-SLP
Rebecca Halsey-Schmidt, MS, CCC-SLP
Cheryl L. Hock, MA, CCC-SLP
Linda R. Jacobson, MS, CCC-SLP
Sheila R. Kimbrough, MS, CCC-SLP
Susan M. Kwass, MS, CCC-SLP
Vivain A. Lewis, MS, CCC-SLP
Peg Major, BS
Laura Mueller, MS, CCC-SLP
Julie A. Petrie, MS, CCC-SLP
Linda Porosky , MS, CCC-SLP
Amy Warda Rivera, BSE
Mary M. Rouleau, MS, CCC-SLP
Dena S. Rubnitz, MS, CCC-SLP
Elaine M. Sathe, MS
Bette N. Vangen
Anne M. Wallschlaeger, MS, CCC-SLP

SOUTH
ALABAMA
Birmingham
Nancy Rentschler, MS, CCC-SLP
Clanton
Karen Davis, MA, BSW
Connie Sellers, BA
Vivian Smith, MA-SLP
Jemison
Deanna Clements, MA, SLP
Lee Ann Jackson, MS, CCC-SLP
Maplesville
Amy P. Conn, MS, CCC-SLP
Shelley Jones, MEd, CCC-SLP

Mobile
Rosanne L. Morisani, MS
Montevallo
Carol Lott, EdS, CCC-SLP
Thorsby
Shelly Cofer, MA, CCC-SLP
Verbena
Sue Ellen Gilliland, BS
ARKANSAS
El Dorado
Debra Calaway-Hammond, MA, CCC-SLP
Hot Springs
Joy Amason, MS, CCC-SLP
Dana Blancaflor, MS, CCC-SLP
C. Suzanne Butler, MA, CCC-SLP
Cindy Davis, MA, CCC-SLP
Connie Headley, MS, CCC-SLP
Jill Lammers, MS, CCC-SLP
Leslea Roberts, BS
Regina Smith, BS
Junction City
Sharon Sanderson Purifoy, MA, CCC-SLP
DELAWARE
New Castle
Patricia Oerther, MA, CCC-SLP
FLORIDA
Delray
Eileen Petersen, MS, CCC-SLP
Hialeah
Donna Dumas, MA, CCC-SLP
Renee Falitz, MS, CCC-SLP
Krista Merandi, EdD, CCC-SLP
Lakeland
Lee S. Dean, MA, CCC-SLP
Kristen C. Gonzalez, MS, CCC-SLP
Amy Tyner, MA, CCC-SLP
Miami
Lillian F. Andron, MA
Carla W. Johnson, MS, CCC-SLP
Teranya Shaye Johnson, BS
Nicole M. Moore, MS, SLP-CCC
Kirsten L. Schwarz, BA
Robin D. Wiggins, MA, SLP
North Miami Beach
Lillian F. Andron, MA
Jean Goldenberg, MA, CCC-SLP
Tampa
Jeanne M. Barth, MA, CCC-SLP

GEORGIA
Blue Ridge
Jennie Williams, BS
Ellijay
Jeannette M. Burgess, MS, CCC-SLP
Milledgeville
Sandra Addy, MEd, CCC-SLP
Michele L. Frost, MEd, CCC-SLP
KENTUCKY
Fort Thomas
Mary Lou Simpson, MA, CCC-SLP
Scottsville
Kelley Swallow Wanta, MA
MARYLAND
Belcamp
Fran Townsend, BA
Vanessa Tull, MEd
NORTH CAROLINA
Cullowhee
Melinda Kuehn, MS, CCC-SLP
Hillsborough
Glenda Davis, MA, CCC-SLP
Louisburg
Aletha C. Watson-White, MA,
    CCC-SLP
Elizabeth Scott Winborne, BS
OKLAHOMA
Picher
Beth Whorton, MA, CCC-SLP
TENNESSEE
Nashville
Patricia F. Allen, MS, MAT, CCC-
    SLP
Christy Harrell, MS, CCC-SLP
Beth Urbanczyk, MS, CCC-SLP
TEXAS
Crosby
Nancy Besly, MA, CCC-SLP, RPED
Ferris
Nancy K. Estes, MA, CCC-SLP
Schulenburg
Charlene Muras, MEd, CCC-SLP
VIRGINIA
Saxe
Elizabeth M. Peaden, BS

WEST
CALIFORNIA
Dixon
Barbara Cringle, MA-SLP

Dos Palos
Michelle Derr, MA, CCC-SLP
Cheryl Williams, MA, CCC-SLP
Folsom
Jan Livingston, MA, CCC-SLP
Christine Richardson, MA
Janice Willing, MA, CCC-SLP
Magalia
Linda C. Stimson, MS, CCC-SLP
Novato
Alexandra Nelson, MA, CCC-SLP
Oroville
Nora Burnham, MA, CCC-SLP
Carla M. Hulfish, MA, CCC-SLP
Susan J. Neben, MA, CCC-SLP
Laura Thomas, MS, CCC-SLP
Sarah J. VonBerg, MA, CCC-SLP
Panorama City
Speech Pathology Staff, Kaiser
    Permanente Outpatient Clinic
Salinas
Rose M. Alvarado, BA, BCAC
San Mateo
Anna L. Strow, MS, CCC-SLP
COLORADO
Littleton
Melissa Dyer, MS, CCC-SLP
Linda A. Gardiner, MA, CCC-SLP
Phyllis Lemon, MS, CCC-SLP
NEW MEXICO
Fruitland
Cheryl Oelze Calvert, MS, CCC-
    SLP
Newcomb
Hubert P. Miller, MA, SLP
Shiprock
Anne Current, MS, CCC-SLP
Mary Ann Greene, MA, CCC-SLP
Brenda J. Tooley, MA, CCC-SLP
NEVADA
Las Vegas
Sharon Dietz, MS, CCC-SLP
OREGON
Aloha
Val Skordal, MA, CCC-SLP
Hillsboro
Melanie Peters, MA, CCC-SLP
Deon Shope, MA, CCC-SLP
UTAH
Cedar City
Vickey J. Carlson, MA, CCC-SLP

WASHINGTON
Kennewick
Susan M. Bruemmer, MS, CCC-SLP

Test Sites

NORTHEAST
CONNECTICUT
Orange
Foundation School
Stamford
The Children's School
MASSACHUSETTS
Boston
Robbins Speech, Language &
    Hearing Center at Emerson
    College
New Bedford
New Bedford Public Schools
Sara D. Ottiwell Elementary School
NEW HAMPSHIRE
Manchester
Webster Elementary School
NEW JERSEY
Howell
Aldrich School
Newbury School
Ramtown School
Southard Elementary School
Taunton School
Milltown
Joyce Kilmer School
Parkview School
Shrewsbury
Coastal Speech Pathology
    Association
NEW YORK
Albertson
Meadow Drive School
Alexander
Alexander Central School
Amherst
Cantalician Center for Learning -
    Preschool Site
Brooklyn
Magen David Yeshivah
Buffalo
Poplar Academy
Commack
Leeway School District

Oceanside
Walter S. Boardman Elementary School
Poughkeepsie
Astor Early Childhood Program
Red Hook
Astor Early Childhood Program
Rifton
Anna Devine Elementary School
Rochester
Lakeshore School
Sayville
Leeway School
Sherman
Sherman Central School
Tappan
W.O. Schaefer Elementary School
PENNSYLVANIA
Franklin
Franklin High School
Franklin Middle School
Polk Elementary School
Sandycreek Elementary School
Perryopolis
Central Elementary School
Frazier Middle School
Perry Elementary School

NORTH CENTRAL
ILLINOIS
Chicago
Chicago Pubilc Schools Demonstration Center
East Moline
Moline School District #40
Fulton
Fulton Elementary School
Lexington
Lexington Elementary School
Normal
BroMenn Healthcare
Norridge
Norridge School District #80
Oakbrook Terrace
West Suburban Speech Clinic
Pleasant Plains
A-C Central Elementary School
Farmingdale Elementary School
Pontiac
OSF Saint James Rehabilitation
Pontiac Township High School

Skokie
Skokie School District #68
INDIANA
East Chicago
East Chicago Public Schools
Franklin Elementary School
Saint Mary's
Saint Stanislaus
Evansville
Early Childhood Program
Evansville-Vanderburgh Early Childhood Program
The Rehabilitation Center
KANSAS
Kansas City
Lamb Early Childhood Center, USD 500
Lamb Early Childhood Special Education Program
Lamb Preschool at Donnelly College
Wichita
Caldwell Elementary School
Cloud Elementary School
Dodge-Edison Partnership School
Lawrence Elementary School
Peterson Elementary School
Rea Woodman Elementary School
Wichita Public Schools
MICHIGAN
Clinton
Clinton Elementary School
Fruitport
Shettler Elementary School
Hillsdale
J.W. Mauck Elementary School
Muskegon
Beach Elementary School
Ravenna
Ravenna Public Schools
Spring Lake
Spring Lake High School
MINNISOTA
Delano
Delano Elementary School
OHIO
Bedford
Glendale Primary School
Fairview Park
Coffinberry Early Education School
Garnett Primary School

Parkview Intermediate School
SOUTH DAKOTA
Kyle
Little Wound District School
Lennox
Lennox Public Schools
Manderson
Wounded Knee District School
Rapid City
Children's Care Hospital and School Outreach
Wakonda
Wakonda Public Schools
WISCONSIN
Markesan
Markesan School District
Milwaukee
65th Street School
A.E. Burdich School
A.F. Doerfler Elementary School
Barton Elementary School
Benjamin Franklin Elementary School
Clement Avenue School
Congress Extended Year-Round School
Craig Montessori School
Custer High School
Fernwood School
Garfield Avenue Elementary School
Grantosa Drive School
Granville Elementary School
Greenfield Montessori School
Jeremiah Curtin Elementary School
John Muir Middle School
Keefe Avenue School
MacDowell Montessori School
Manitoba School
Marshall High School
Milwaukee Public Schools
Morgandale Elementary School
Morse Middle School
Nebraska School
Riverside University High School
Rufus King High School
Sarah Scott Middle School for the Health Sciences
Sholes Middle School
South Division High School
Whitman Elementary School
Thoreau Elementary School

SOUTH
ALABAMA
Birmingham
Cahaba Heights Community School
Clanton
Chilton County Board of Education
Clanton Elementary School
Jemison
Jemison Elementary School
Jemison Middle School
Maplesville
Isabella High School
Maplesville High School
Mobile
St. Ignatius Day Care
Woodcock Elementary School
Montevallo
Montevallo Child Study Center
Thorsby
Thorsby High School
Verbena
Verbena High School
ARKANSAS
El Dorado
Parkers Chapel Elementary School
Hot Springs
First Step, Inc.
Junction City
Junction City Public Schools
DELAWARE
New Castle
Wallace Wallin School
FLORIDA
Delray
Banyan Creek Elementary School
Hialeah
Earnest Graham Elementary School
Hialeah Elementary School
Hialeah Middle School
Jose Marti Middle School
Miami Lakes Elementary School
Lakeland
Central Florida Speech & Hearing
  Center
Miami
Andrea Draizar, PhD & Associates
Crestview Elementary School
Dade County Public Schools
George Washington Carver Middle
  School
Mays Middle School

Miami Norland Middle School
Mount Herman A.M.E.
Myrtle Grove Elementary
Phyllis Ruth Miller Elementary
  School
Rockway Elementary School
Rockway Middle School
Silver Bluff Elementary School
Westview Elementary School
Westview Middle School
North Miami Beach
Samuel Scheck Hillel Community
  Day School
Toras Chaim High School
Toras Emes Academy
Toras Emes Early Childhood
  Education
Sebastian
Indian River School Board
Tampa
JMB Speech Language Pathology
  Services, Inc.
GEORGIA
Blue Ridge
Fannin County School District
Ellijay
Ellijay Primary School
Gilmer Middle School
Milledgeville
Blandy Elementary School
Creekside Elementary School
Southside Elementary School
KENTUCKY
Fort Thomas
Highlands High School
Robert D. Johnson Elementary
  School
Scottsville
Allen County Schools
MARYLAND
Belcamp
Church Creek Elementary School
NORTH CAROLINA
Cullowhee
Western Carolina University
Hillsborough
Central Elementary School
Louisburg
Bunn Middle School
Edward Best Elementary School
Laurel Mill Elementary School

Louisburg High School
Terrell Lane Middle School
OKLAHOMA
Picher
Picher-Cardin Elementary School
TENNESSEE
Nashville
Madison School
Pi Beta Phi Rehabilitation Institute
TEXAS
Crosby
Crosby Independent School
  District
Ferris
Ferris Elementary School
Schulenburg
Schulenburg/Flatonia Special
  Education School
VIRGINIA
Charlotte Court House
Randolph-Henry High School
Saxe
Bacon District Elementary School

WEST
ARIZONA
Phoenix
Heatherbrae Elementary School
CALIFORNIA
Berkeley
El Cerrito Preschool
Castro Valley
Redwood Christian School
Dixon
Tremont Elementary School
Dos Palos
Dos Palos High School
Folsom
Blanche Sprentz Elementary
  School
Folsom-Cordova Unified School
  District
Mills Middle Middle School
Theodore Judah Elementary School
Magalia
Pines Elementary School
Mill Valley
Robin's Nest Preschool
Novato
Lynwood Elementary School
Miss Sandie's School

Oroville
Acacia Speech
Butte County Office of Education
First United Methodist Church State
    Preschool
Oakdale Heights School
Poplar Avenue Elementary School
Panorama City
Kaiser Permanente Outpatient
    Clinic
Petaluma
Petaluma Valley Day School
Salinas
Bardin Elementary School
San Anselmo
Robin's Nest Preschool
San Lorenzo
Redwood Christian High School
San Mateo
Horrall Elementary School

Laurel Elementary School
COLORADO
Littleton
Lenski Elementary School
Peabody Elementary School
NEW MEXICO
Fruitland
Ojo Amarillo Elementary School
Newcomb
Newcomb Elementary School
Roswell
Roswell Independent School
    District
Shiprock
Central Consolidated School
    District #22
Nataani Nez Elementary School
Nizhoni Elementary School

Tse Bit'Ai Middle School
NEVADA
Las Vegas
K.O. Knudson Middle School
OREGON
Aloha
Butternut Creek Elementary School
Hillsboro
Eastwood Elementary School
Indian HIlls Elementary School
UTAH
Cedar City
Feddlers Elementary School
Iron County School District
WASHINGTON
Kennewick
Certified Speech-Language
    Services

Demographic Characteristics of Samples in Validity Studies

This appendix lists the demographic characteristics of samples for whom validity data is reported in Tables 8.1 through 8.6. Samples are listed in alphabetical order. Samples identified by test name are listed first and followed by samples identified by exceptional group name.

Test Comparison Samples
Data for these samples appear in Tables 8.1–8.5.

CAT5 sample (*N*=41)
Age: min.=7-4 years; max.=12-10 years; median=8-8 years
Region: North Central, 41 (100.0%)
Race/Ethnicity: Hispanic, 1 (2.4%); White, 40 (97.6%)
Gender: Female, 22 (53.7%); Male, 19 (46.3%)
Parent Education: Grade 11 or less, 3 (7.3%); High School, 12 (29.3%); 1-3 Years College, 18 (43.9%); 4+ Years College, 8 (19.5%)
Residence: Urban, 36 (87.8%); Rural, 5 (12.2%)
Educational Classification: Regular Ed., 36 (87.8%); Special Ed., 5 (12.2%)

CELF-3 sample (*N*=50)
Age: min.=5-10 years; max.=18-4 years; median=9-8 years
Region: Northeast, 21 (42.0%); North Central, 17 (34.0%); South, 10 (20.0%); West, 2 (4.0%)
Race/Ethnicity: Asian, 1 (2.0%); Black, 7 (14.0%); Hispanic, 3 (6.0%); White, 37 (74.0%); Other, 2 (4.0%)
Gender: Female, 22 (44.0%); Male, 28 (56.0%)
Parent Education: Grade 11 or less, 8 (16.0%); High School, 19 (38.0%); 1-3 Years College, 11 (22.0%); 4+ Years College, 12 (24.0%)
Residence: Urban, 40 (80.0%); Rural, 10 (20.0%)
Educational Classification: Regular Ed., 10 (20.0%); Special Ed., 40 (80.0%)

EOWPVT (1979) sample (*N*=67)
Age: min.=3-7 years; max.=14-8 years; median=7-5 years
Region: Northeast, 18 (26.9%); North Central, 33 (49.3%); South, 9 (13.4%); West, 7 (10.4%)
Race/Ethnicity: Asian, 2 (3.0%); Black, 8 (11.9%); Hispanic, 5 (7.5%); White, 52 (77.6%)
Gender: Female, 21 (31.3%); Male, 46 (68.7%)
Parent Education: Grade 11 or less, 6 (9.0%); High School, 22 (32.8%); 1-3 Years College, 23 (34.3%); 4+ Years College, 16 (23.9%)
Residence: Urban, 43 (64.2%); Rural, 24 (35.8%)

Educational Classification: Regular Ed., 28 (41.8%); Special Ed., 39 (58.2%)

EOWPVT-R (1990) sample (*N*=94)
Age: min.=2-4 years; max.=13-10 years; median=5-9 years
Region: Northeast, 18 (19.1%); North Central, 34 (36.2%); South, 37 (39.4%); West, 5 (5.3%)
Race/Ethnicity: Asian, 2 (2.1%); Black, 36 (38.2%); Hispanic, 13 (13.8%); White, 43 (45.7%)
Gender: Female, 39 (41.5%); Male, 55 (58.5%)
Parent Education: Grade 11 or less, 26 (27.7%); High School, 19 (20.2%); 1-3 Years College, 30 (31.9%); 4+ Years College, 19 (20.2%)
Residence: Urban, 63 (67.0%); Rural, 31 (33.0%)
Educational Classification: Regular Ed., 23 (24.5%); Special Ed., 71 (75.5%)

EVT sample (*N*=26)
Age: min.=3-7 years; max.=16-7 years; median=10-3 years
Region: Northeast, 18 (69.2%); North Central, 4 (15.3%); South, 3 (11.5%); West, 1 (3.8%)
Race/Ethnicity: Asian, 2 (7.7%); Black, 2 (7.7%); Hispanic, 1 (3.8%); White, 21 (80.8%)
Gender: Female, 12 (46.2%); Male, 14 (53.8%)
Parent Education: Grade 11 or less, 2 (7.7%); High School, 13 (50.0%); 1-3 Years College, 2 (7.7%); 4+ Years College, 9 (34.6%)
Residence: Urban, 21 (80.8%); Rural, 5 (19.2%)
Educational Classification: Regular Ed., 5 (19.2%); Special Ed., 21 (80.8%)

MAT7 sample (*N*=23)
Age: min.=12-11 years; max.=14-10 years; median=14-0 years
Region: North Central, 23 (100.0%)
Race/Ethnicity: Hispanic, 1 (4.3%); White, 22 (95.7%)
Gender: Female, 13 (56.5%); Male, 10 (43.5%)
Parent Education: Grade 11 or less, 1 (4.3%); High School, 6 (26.1%); 1-3 Years College, 8 (34.8%); 4+ Years College, 8 (34.8%)
Residence: Urban, 23 (100.0%)
Educational Classification: Regular Ed., 23 (100.0%)

OLSAT-7 sample (N=40)

Age: min.=7-7 years; max.=17-7 years; median=13-10 years

Region: North Central, 40 (100.0%)

Race/Ethnicity: Asian, 2 (5.0%); Hispanic, 1 (2.5%); White, 37 (92.5%)

Gender: Female, 23 (57.5%); Male, 17 (42.5%)

Parent Education: Grade 11 or less, 1 (2.5%); High School, 6 (15.0%); 1-3 Years College, 15 (37.5%); 4+ Years College, 18 (45.0%)

Residence: Urban, 29 (72.5%); Rural, 11 (27.5%)

Educational Classification: Regular Ed., 38 (95.0%); Special Ed., 2 (5.0%)

OWLS sample (N=35)

Age: min.=3-1 years; max.=14-3 years; median=8-1 years

Region: Northeast, 10 (28.6%); North Central, 14 (40.0%); South, 10 (28.6%); West, 1 (2.8%)

Race/Ethnicity: Black, 3 (8.6%); Hispanic, 2 (5.7%); White, 25 (71.4%); Other, 5 (14.3%)

Gender: Female, 14 (40.0%); Male, 21 (60.0%)

Parent Education: Grade 11 or less, 10 (28.6%); High School, 15 (42.8%); 1-3 Years College, 7 (20.0%); 4+ Years College, 3 (8.6%)

Residence: Urban, 19 (54.3%); Rural, 16 (45.7%)

Educational Classification: Regular Ed., 9 (25.7%); Special Ed., 26 (74.3%)

PLS-3 sample (N=59)

Age: min.=2-4 years; max.=10-0 years; median=4-11 years

Region: Northeast, 13 (22.0%); North Central, 35 (59.3%); South, 9 (15.3%); West, 2 (3.4%)

Race/Ethnicity: Asian, 2 (3.4%); Black, 13 (22.0%); Hispanic, 5 (8.5%); White, 39 (66.1%)

Gender: Female, 18 (30.5%); Male, 41 (69.5%)

Parent Education: Grade 11 or less, 15 (25.4%); High School, 16 (27.1%); 1-3 Years College, 12 (20.4%); 4+ Years College, 16 (27.1%)

Residence: Urban, 45 (76.3%); Rural, 14 (23.7%)

Educational Classification: Regular Ed., 13 (22.0%); Special Ed., 46 (78.0%)

PPVT-R sample (N=31)

Age: min.=3-7 years; max.=12-1 years; median=7-5 years

Region: Northeast, 7 (22.6%); North Central, 19 (61.3%); South, 4 (12.9%); West, 1 (3.2%)

Race/Ethnicity: Asian, 1 (3.2%); Black, 3 (9.7%); White, 27 (87.1%)

Gender: Female, 11 (35.5%); Male, 20 (64.5%)

Parent Education: Grade 11 or less, 2 (6.5%); High School, 8 (25.8%); 1-3 Years College, 10 (32.2%); 4+ Years College, 11 (35.5%)

Residence: Urban, 17 (54.8%); Rural, 14 (45.2%)

Educational Classification: Regular Ed., 8 (25.8%); Special Ed., 23 (74.2%)

PPVT-III sample (N=67)

Age: min.=3-7 years; max.=18-11 years; median=9-4 years

Region: Northeast, 36 (53.7%); North Central, 10 (14.9%); South, 4 (6.0%); West, 17 (25.4%)

Race/Ethnicity: Asian, 2 (3.0%); Black, 7 (10.4%); Hispanic, 5 (7.5%); White, 51 (76.1%); Other, 2 (3.0%)

Gender: Female, 22 (32.8%); Male, 45 (67.2%)

Parent Education: Grade 11 or less, 4 (6.0%); High School, 24 (35.8%); 1-3 Years College, 13 (19.4%); 4+ Years College, 26 (38.8%)

Residence: Urban, 44 (65.7%); Rural, 23 (34.3%)

Educational Classification: Regular Ed., 17 (25.4%); Special Ed., 50 (74.6%)

ROWPVT sample (N=2,327)

See description of the standardization sample, Tables 6.2–6.4.

SAT9 sample (N=53)

Age: min.=8-8 years; max.=18-8 years; median=12-11 years

Region: North Central, 6 (11.3%); South, 21 (39.6%); West, 26 (49.1%)

Race/Ethnicity: Asian, 2 (3.8%); Black, 4 (7.5%); Hispanic, 3 (5.7%); White, 43 (81.1%); Other, 1 (1.9%)

Gender: Female, 25 (47.2%); Male, 28 (52.8%)

Parent Education: Grade 11 or less, 8 (15.1%); High School, 17 (32.1%); 1-3 Years College, 10 (18.8%); 4+ Years College, 18 (34.0%)

Residence: Urban, 47 (88.7%); Rural, 6 (11.3%)

Educational Classification: Regular Ed., 51 (96.2%); Special Ed., 2 (3.8%)

SB-4th Ed. sample (*N*=19)
Age: min.=5-5 years; max.=12-1 years; median=7-0 years
Region: Northeast, 6 (31.6%); North Central, 8 (42.1%); South, 5 (26.3%)
Race/Ethnicity: Black, 7 (36.8%); Hispanic, 3 (15.8%); White, 9 (47.4%)
Gender: Female, 9 (47.4%); Male, 10 (52.6%)
Parent Education: Grade 11 or less, 2 (10.5%); High School, 6 (31.6%); 1-3 Years College, 7 (36.8%); 4+ Years College, 4 (21.1%)
Residence: Urban, 12 (63.2%); Rural, 7 (36.8%)
Educational Classification: Regular Ed., 1 (5.3%); Special Ed., 18 (94.7%)

TACL-R sample (*N*=31)
Age: min.=3-7 years; max.=10-3 years; median=5-1 years
Region: Northeast, 8 (25.8%); North Central, 2 (6.5%); South, 21 (67.7%)
Race/Ethnicity: Black, 14 (45.2%); Hispanic, 3 (9.7%); White, 12 (38.7%); Other, 2 (6.4%)
Gender: Female, 10 (32.3%); Male, 21 (67.7%)
Parent Education: Grade 11 or less, 5 (16.1%); High School, 7 (22.6%); 1-3 Years College, 13 (41.9%); 4+ Years College, 6 (19.4%)
Residence: Urban, 29 (93.5%); Rural, 2 (6.5%)
Educational Classification: Regular Ed., 6 (19.4%); Special Ed., 25 (80.6%)

TOLD-P:3 sample (*N*=28)
Age: min.=5-4 years; max.=10-3 years; median=6-7 years
Region: Northeast, 15 (53.6%); North Central, 3 (10.7%); South, 3 (10.7%); West, 7 (25.0%)
Race/Ethnicity: Asian, 1 (3.6%); Black, 2 (7.1%); Hispanic, 1 (3.6%); White, 24 (85.7%)
Gender: Female, 7 (25.0%); Male, 21 (75.0%)
Parent Education: Grade 11 or less, 3 (10.7%); High School, 3 (10.7%); 1-3 Years College, 10 (35.7%); 4+ Years College, 12 (42.9%)
Residence: Urban, 27 (96.4%); Rural, 1 (3.6%)
Educational Classification: Regular Ed., 13 (46.4%); Special Ed., 15 (53.6%)

WJ-R sample (*N*=21)
Age: min.=7-2 years; max.=14-10 years; median=9-1 years

Region: North Central, 14 (66.7%); South, 6 (28.5%); West, 1 (4.8%)
Race/Ethnicity: Black, 3 (14.2%); White, 17 (81.0%); Other, 1 (4.8%)
Gender: Female, 5 (23.8%); Male, 16 (76.2%)
Parent Education: Grade 11 or less, 3 (14.3%); High School, 10 (47.6%); 1-3 Years College, 3 (14.3%); 4+ Years College, 5 (23.8%)
Residence: Urban, 14 (66.7%); Rural, 7 (33.3%)
Educational Classification: Regular Ed., 3 (14.3%); Special Ed., 18 (85.7%)

WISC-III sample (*N*=48)
Age: min.=7-1 years; max.=15-9 years; median=9-9 years
Region: Northeast, 5 (10.4%); North Central, 23 (47.9%); South, 14 (29.2%); West, 6 (12.5%)
Race/Ethnicity: Black, 7 (14.6%); Hispanic, 2 (4.2%); White, 37 (77.0%); Other, 2 (4.2%)
Gender: Female, 18 (37.5%); Male, 30 (62.5%)
Parent Education: Grade 11 or less, 10 (20.8%); High School, 18 (37.5%); 1-3 Years College, 9 (18.8%); 4+ Years College, 11 (22.9%)
Residence: Urban, 36 (75.0%); Rural, 12 (25.0%)
Educational Classification: Regular Ed., 9 (18.8%); Special Ed., 39 (81.3%)

Exceptional Group Samples
Data for these samples appear in Table 8.6.

ADHD/ADD sample (*N*=21)
Age: min.=4-11 years; max.=16-9 years; median=9-5 years
Region: Northeast, 7 (33.3%); North Central, 6 (28.6%); South, 6 (28.6%); West, 2 (9.5%)
Race/Ethnicity: Black, 1 (4.8%); Hispanic, 2 (9.5%); White, 18 (85.7%)
Gender: Female, 3 (14.3%); Male, 18 (85.7%)
Parent Education: Grade 11 or less, 1 (4.8%); High School, 7 (33.3%); 1-3 Years College, 5 (23.8%); 4+ Years College, 8 (38.1%)
Residence: Urban, 17 (81.0%); Rural, 4 (19.0%)

Articulation sample (*N*=327)

Age: min.=2-5 years; max.=16-10 years; median=7-7 years

Region: Northeast, 76 (23.2%); North Central, 126 (38.5%); South, 87 (26.7%); West, 38 (11.6%)

Race/Ethnicity: Asian, 4 (1.2%); Black, 26 (8.0%); Hispanic, 23 (7.0%); White, 270 (82.6%); Other, 4 (1.2%)

Gender: Female, 117 (35.8%); Male, 210 (64.2%)

Parent Education: Grade 11 or less, 27 (8.3%); High School, 97 (29.7%); 1-3 Years College, 96 (29.4%); 4+ Years College, 107 (32.7%)

Residence: Urban, 210 (64.2%); Rural, 117 (35.8%)

Auditory Processing Deficit sample (*N*=28)

Age: min.=4-3 years; max.=14-1 years; median=10-1 years

Region: Northeast, 15 (53.6%); North Central, 7 (25.0%); South, 4 (14.3%); West, 2 (7.1%)

Race/Ethnicity: Black, 4 (14.3%); Hispanic, 2 (7.1%); White, 22 (78.6%)

Gender: Female, 11 (39.3%); Male, 17 (60.7%)

Parent Education: Grade 11 or less, 3 (10.7%); High School, 8 (28.6%); 1-3 Years College, 8 (28.6%); 4+ Years College, 9 (32.1%)

Residence: Urban, 24 (85.7%); Rural, 4 (14.3%)

Autistic sample (*N*=35)

Age: min.=4-10 years; max.=18-1 years; median=11-8 years

Region: Northeast, 30 (85.7%); North Central, 1 (2.9%); South, 2 (5.7%); West, 2 (5.7%)

Race/Ethnicity: Asian, 2 (5.7%); Black, 1 (2.9%); Hispanic, 1 (2.9%); White, 31 (88.5%)

Gender: Female, 5 (14.3%); Male, 30 (85.7%)

Parent Education: High School, 13 (37.1%); 1-3 Years College, 2 (5.7%); 4+ Years College, 20 (57.2%)

Residence: Urban, 32 (91.4%); Rural, 3 (8.6%)

Behavioral Disorder sample (*N*=19)

Age: min.=3-0 years; max.=13-7 years; median=5-2 years

Region: Northeast, 5 (26.3%); North Central, 7 (36.9%); South, 5 (26.3%); West, 2 (10.5%)

Race/Ethnicity: Black, 5 (26.3%); Hispanic, 1 (5.3%); White, 13 (68.4%)

Gender: Female, 5 (26.3%); Male, 14 (73.7%)

Parent Education: Grade 11 or less, 5 (26.3%); High School, 4 (21.1%); 1-3 Years College, 6 (31.5%); 4+ Years College, 4 (21.1%)

Residence: Urban, 14 (73.7%); Rural, 5 (26.3%)

Exp./Rec. Language Disorder sample (*N*=141)

Age: min.=2-4 years; max.=14-10 years; median=7-5 years

Region: Northeast, 64 (45.4%); North Central, 47 (33.3%); South, 6 (4.3%); West, 24 (17.0%)

Race/Ethnicity: Asian, 3 (2.1%); Black, 15 (10.6%); Hispanic, 12 (8.5%); White, 109 (77.4%); Other, 2 (1.4%)

Gender: Female, 43 (30.5%); Male, 98 (69.5%)

Parent Education: Grade 11 or less, 19 (13.5%); High School, 46 (32.6%); 1-3 Years College, 30 (21.3%); 4+ Years College, 46 (32.6%)

Residence: Urban, 127 (90.1%); Rural, 14 (9.9%)

Fluency Disorder sample (*N*=31)

Age: min.=3-7 years; max.=18-8 years; median=8-9 years

Region: Northeast, 4 (12.9%); North Central, 11 (35.5%); South, 13 (41.9%); West, 3 (9.7%)

Race/Ethnicity: Asian, 1 (3.2%); Black, 11 (35.5%); Hispanic, 5 (16.1%); White, 14 (45.2%)

Gender: Female, 3 (9.7%); Male, 28 (90.3%)

Parent Education: Grade 11 or less, 1 (3.2%); High School, 5 (16.2%); 1-3 Years College, 16 (51.6%); 4+ Years College, 9 (29.0%)

Residence: Urban, 28 (90.3%); Rural, 3 (9.7%)

Hearing Loss sample (*N*=19)

Age: min.=4-4 years; max.=14-5 years; median=8-5 years

Region: Northeast, 1 (5.3%); North Central, 9 (47.4%); South, 8 (42.0%); West, 1 (5.3%)

Race/Ethnicity: Black, 2 (10.5%); White, 17 (89.5%)

Gender: Female, 11 (57.9%); Male, 8 (42.1%)

Parent Education: High School, 3 (15.8%); 1-3 Years College, 5 (26.3%); 4+ Years College, 11 (57.9%)

Residence: Urban, 17 (89.5%); Rural, 2 (10.5%)

Language Delay sample (*N*=208)

Age: min.=2-0 years; max.=16-7 years; median=6-10 years

Region: Northeast, 50 (24.0%); North Central, 46

(22.1%); South, 99 (47.6%); West, 13 (6.3%)

Race/Ethnicity: Asian, 1 (0.5%); Black, 57 (27.4%); Hispanic, 14 (6.7%); White, 130 (62.5%); Other, 6 (2.9%)

Gender: Female, 74 (35.6%); Male, 134 (64.4%)

Parent Education: Grade 11 or less, 43 (20.7%); High School, 62 (29.8%); 1-3 Years College, 58 (27.9%); 4+ Years College, 45 (21.6%)

Residence: Urban, 154 (74.0%); Rural, 54 (26.0%)

Learning Disabled sample (*N*=143)

Age: min.=3-6 years; max.=18-3 years; median=9-10 years

Region: Northeast, 35 (24.5%); North Central, 41 (28.6%); South, 46 (32.2%); West, 21 (14.7%)

Race/Ethnicity: Asian, 3 (2.1%); Black, 18 (12.6%); Hispanic, 12 (8.4%); White, 105 (73.4%); Other, 5 (3.5%)

Gender: Female, 47 (32.9%); Male, 96 (67.1%)

Parent Education: Grade 11 or less, 24 (16.7%); High School, 46 (32.2%); 1-3 Years College, 46 (32.2%); 4+ Years College, 27 (18.9%)

Residence: Urban, 107 (74.8%); Rural, 36 (25.2%)

Mentally Retarded sample (*N*=51)

Age: min.=3-6 years; max.=18-11 years; median=10-9 years

Region: Northeast, 11 (21.5%); North Central, 13 (25.5%); South, 26 (51.0%); West, 1 (2.0%)

Race/Ethnicity: Black, 9 (17.6%); Hispanic, 7 (13.7%); White, 35 (68.7%)

Gender: Female, 25 (49.0%); Male, 26 (51.0%)

Parent Education: Grade 11 or less, 12 (23.5%); High School, 24 (47.1%); 1-3 Years College, 11 (21.6%); 4+ Years College, 4 (7.8%)

Residence: Urban, 27 (52.9%); Rural, 24 (47.1%)

APPENDIX D

NORMS TABLES

Raw Score	2-0	2-1	2-2	2-3	2-4	2-5
1	59	57	55	<55		
2	62	60	58	56	<55	<55
3	66	64	61	59	57	56
4	69	67	64	62	60	58
5	72	69	67	64	62	60
6	74	72	69	66	64	62
7	77	74	72	69	67	64
8	79	76	74	71	69	66
9	81	78	76	73	71	68
10	83	81	78	76	74	71
11	85	83	80	78	76	73
12	87	85	83	81	78	76
13	89	87	85	83	81	79
14	92	90	88	86	84	82
15	94	92	90	89	87	85
16	96	94	92	90	89	87
17	97	96	94	92	91	89
18	99	98	96	94	93	91
19	101	99	98	96	94	93
20	102	100	99	97	95	94
21	103	102	100	99	97	96
22	105	104	102	101	99	98
23	106	105	103	102	100	99
24	108	106	105	104	102	101
25	109	107	106	105	103	102
26	110	109	107	106	104	103
27	112	110	109	108	106	105
28	113	111	110	109	107	106
29	114	113	111	110	108	107
30	115	114	112	111	109	108

Raw Score	2-0	2-1	2-2	2-3	2-4	2-5
31	117	115	114	113	111	110
32	118	116	115	114	112	111
33	119	117	116	115	113	112
34	120	119	117	116	114	113
35	121	120	118	117	115	114
36	123	122	120	119	117	116
37	124	123	121	120	118	117
38	126	124	123	121	119	118
39	127	125	124	122	120	119
40	129	127	126	124	122	121
41	130	128	127	125	123	122
42	131	130	128	126	125	123
43	132	131	129	127	126	124
44	134	133	131	129	128	126
45	136	134	132	130	129	127
46	137	135	133	131	130	128
47	138	137	135	133	132	130
48	140	138	136	134	133	131
49	141	139	137	136	134	132
50	143	141	139	137	136	134
51	144	143	141	139	138	136
52	>145	144	142	140	139	137
53		>145	144	142	141	139
54			145	143	142	140
55			>145	145	144	142
56				>145	>145	144
57						145
58						>145
59						
60						

Raw Score	2-6	2-7	2-8	2-9	2-10	2-11
1						
2						
3	<55	<55				
4	56	55	<55	<55		
5	58	57	56	55	<55	<55
6	60	59	58	57	56	55
7	62	61	60	59	58	57
8	64	63	62	61	60	59
9	66	65	64	63	62	61
10	69	68	67	66	65	64
11	71	70	69	68	67	66
12	74	73	72	71	69	68
13	77	76	74	73	72	70
14	80	79	77	76	74	73
15	83	82	80	78	77	75
16	85	84	82	80	79	77
17	87	86	84	82	81	79
18	89	87	86	84	82	80
19	91	89	88	86	84	82
20	92	91	89	87	86	84
21	94	93	91	89	88	86
22	96	95	93	91	90	88
23	97	96	94	92	91	89
24	99	98	96	94	93	91
25	100	99	97	96	94	93
26	101	100	98	97	96	94
27	103	102	100	99	98	96
28	104	103	101	100	99	97
29	105	104	103	101	100	99
30	106	105	104	102	101	100
31	108	107	106	104	103	102
32	109	108	107	105	104	103
33	110	109	108	107	105	104
34	111	110	109	108	106	105
35	112	111	110	109	107	106
36	114	113	112	111	109	108
37	115	114	113	112	110	109
38	116	115	114	113	111	110
39	117	116	115	114	113	112
40	119	118	117	116	114	113
41	120	119	118	117	115	114
42	121	120	119	118	116	115
43	122	121	120	119	117	116
44	124	123	122	120	119	118
45	125	124	123	122	120	119
46	126	125	124	123	121	120
47	128	127	126	124	123	122
48	129	128	127	125	124	123
49	130	129	128	126	125	124
50	132	131	130	128	127	126
51	134	133	131	130	129	127
52	135	134	132	131	130	128
53	137	136	134	133	131	130
54	138	137	135	134	133	131
55	140	139	137	136	134	133
56	142	141	139	137	136	134
57	143	142	140	138	137	135
58	145	144	142	140	139	137
59	>145	145	143	141	140	138
60		>145	145	143	142	140
61			>145	145	144	142
62				>145	145	143
63					>145	145
64						>145
65						
66						
67						
68						
69						
70						

TABLE D.1—Conversion of Raw Scores to Standard Scores
Ages 3-0–3-5

Raw Score	3-0	3-1	3-2	3-3	3-4	3-5
6	<55	<55				
7	56	55	<55	<55		
8	58	57	56	55	<55	<55
9	60	59	58	57	56	55
10	62	61	60	59	58	57
11	64	63	62	61	60	59
12	67	66	64	63	62	61
13	69	67	66	65	63	62
14	71	70	68	67	65	64
15	74	72	71	69	67	66
16	75	74	72	70	69	67
17	77	76	74	72	71	69
18	79	77	75	73	72	70
19	81	79	77	75	74	72
20	82	81	79	77	76	74
21	84	83	81	79	78	76
22	86	85	83	81	80	78
23	88	86	85	83	81	80
24	90	88	87	85	83	82
25	91	90	88	87	85	84
26	93	91	90	89	87	86
27	95	93	92	91	89	88
28	96	94	93	92	90	89
29	97	96	95	93	92	91
30	98	97	96	94	93	92
31	100	99	98	96	95	94
32	101	100	99	97	96	95
33	103	102	100	99	98	97
34	104	103	101	100	99	98
35	105	104	102	101	100	99
36	107	106	104	103	102	101
37	108	107	105	104	103	102
38	109	108	106	105	104	103
39	110	109	108	107	106	105
40	112	111	109	108	107	106
41	113	112	110	109	108	107
42	114	113	111	110	109	108
43	115	114	112	111	110	109
44	116	115	114	112	111	110
45	118	117	115	114	113	112
46	119	118	116	115	114	113
47	120	119	118	116	115	114
48	121	120	119	117	116	115
49	122	121	120	118	117	116
50	124	123	122	120	119	118
51	126	124	123	122	120	119
52	127	125	124	123	121	120
53	128	127	125	124	122	121
54	130	128	127	126	124	123
55	131	130	128	127	125	124
56	133	131	130	128	126	125
57	134	132	131	129	127	126
58	135	134	132	130	129	127
59	137	135	134	132	130	129
60	138	137	135	133	132	130
61	140	139	137	135	134	132
62	141	140	138	136	135	133
63	143	142	140	138	137	135
64	145	143	141	139	138	136
65	>145	145	143	141	140	138
66		>145	145	143	142	140
67			>145	145	144	142
68				>145	145	143
69					>145	145
70						>145
71						
72						
73						
74						
75						

TABLE D.1—Conversion of Raw Scores to Standard Scores
Ages 3-6–3-11

Raw Score	3-6	3-7	3-8	3-9	3-10	3-11
6						
7						
8						
9	<55	<55				
10	56	55	<55	<55	<55	
11	58	57	56	55	55	<55
12	60	59	58	57	57	56
13	61	60	59	59	58	57
14	63	62	61	60	60	59
15	65	64	63	62	62	61
16	66	65	64	63	63	62
17	68	67	66	65	65	64
18	69	68	67	66	66	65
19	71	70	69	68	67	66
20	73	72	71	70	69	68
21	75	74	73	72	71	70
22	76	76	75	74	73	72
23	78	77	76	75	74	73
24	80	79	78	77	76	75
25	82	81	80	79	78	77
26	84	83	82	81	79	78
27	86	85	84	83	81	80
28	87	86	85	84	82	81
29	89	88	87	86	84	83
30	90	89	88	87	85	84
31	92	91	90	89	87	86
32	93	92	91	90	89	88
33	95	94	93	92	90	89
34	96	95	94	93	91	90
35	97	96	95	94	93	92
36	99	98	97	96	94	93
37	100	99	98	97	96	95
38	101	100	99	98	97	96
39	103	102	101	100	99	98
40	104	103	102	101	100	99
41	105	104	103	102	101	100
42	106	105	104	103	102	101
43	107	106	105	104	103	102
44	108	107	106	105	104	103
45	110	109	108	107	106	105

Raw Score	3-6	3-7	3-8	3-9	3-10	3-11
46	111	110	109	108	107	106
47	112	111	110	109	108	107
48	113	112	111	110	109	108
49	114	113	112	111	110	109
50	116	115	114	113	112	111
51	117	116	115	114	113	112
52	118	117	116	115	114	113
53	119	118	117	116	115	114
54	121	120	119	118	117	116
55	122	121	120	119	118	117
56	123	122	121	120	119	118
57	124	123	122	121	120	119
58	125	124	123	122	121	120
59	127	126	125	124	122	121
60	128	127	126	125	124	123
61	130	129	128	127	125	124
62	131	130	129	128	126	125
63	133	132	131	129	128	127
64	134	133	132	130	129	128
65	136	135	134	132	131	130
66	138	137	135	134	133	131
67	140	139	137	136	134	133
68	141	140	138	137	135	134
69	143	142	140	139	137	136
70	145	144	142	140	139	137
71	>145	145	143	141	140	138
72		>145	145	143	142	140
73			>145	145	144	142
74				>145	>145	144
75						145
76						>145
77						
78						
79						
80						
81						
82						
83						
84						
85						

Raw Score	4-0	4-1	4-2	4-3	4-4	4-5
11	<55					
12	55	<55	<55	<55		
13	57	56	55	55	<55	
14	58	57	57	56	55	<55
15	60	59	59	58	57	56
16	61	60	60	59	58	57
17	63	62	62	61	60	59
18	64	63	63	62	61	60
19	66	65	64	63	62	61
20	68	67	66	65	64	63
21	69	68	67	66	65	64
22	71	70	69	68	67	66
23	72	71	70	69	68	67
24	74	73	72	71	70	69
25	75	74	73	72	71	70
26	77	76	74	73	72	71
27	79	78	76	75	74	73
28	80	79	77	76	75	74
29	82	81	79	78	77	76
30	83	82	80	79	78	77
31	85	84	82	81	80	79
32	86	85	84	83	82	81
33	88	87	85	84	83	82
34	89	88	86	85	84	83
35	90	89	88	87	86	85
36	92	91	89	88	87	86
37	93	92	91	90	89	88
38	94	93	92	91	90	89
39	96	95	94	93	92	91
40	97	96	95	94	93	92
41	98	97	96	95	94	93
42	99	98	97	96	95	94
43	101	100	99	98	97	96
44	102	101	100	99	98	97
45	103	102	101	100	99	98
46	105	104	103	102	101	100
47	106	105	104	103	102	101
48	107	106	105	104	103	102
49	108	107	106	105	104	103
50	109	108	107	106	105	104

Raw Score	4-0	4-1	4-2	4-3	4-4	4-5
51	110	109	108	107	106	105
52	111	110	109	108	107	106
53	113	112	111	110	109	108
54	114	113	112	111	110	109
55	115	114	113	112	111	110
56	116	115	114	113	112	111
57	117	116	115	114	113	112
58	118	117	116	115	114	113
59	120	119	117	116	115	114
60	121	120	119	118	117	116
61	123	122	120	119	118	117
62	124	123	121	120	119	118
63	125	124	123	121	120	119
64	126	125	124	122	121	120
65	128	127	126	124	123	122
66	130	128	127	126	124	123
67	131	130	128	127	125	124
68	132	131	129	128	126	125
69	134	133	131	130	128	127
70	136	134	133	131	129	128
71	137	135	134	132	130	129
72	139	137	136	134	132	131
73	140	139	137	135	134	132
74	142	141	139	137	136	134
75	144	142	140	138	137	135
76	>145	144	142	140	139	137
77		>145	144	142	141	139
78			>145	144	143	141
79				145	144	142
80				>145	>145	144
81						>145
82						
83						
84						
85						
86						
87						
88						
89						
90						

Raw Score	4-6	4-7	4-8	4-9	4-10	4-11
11						
12						
13						
14	<55	<55				
15	56	55	<55	<55		
16	57	56	56	55	<55	<55
17	59	58	58	57	56	56
18	60	59	59	58	57	57
19	61	60	60	59	58	58
20	63	62	62	61	60	60
21	64	63	63	62	61	61
22	65	64	64	63	62	62
23	66	65	65	64	63	63
24	68	67	66	66	65	64
25	69	68	67	67	66	65
26	70	69	68	68	67	66
27	72	71	70	70	69	68
28	73	72	71	71	70	69
29	75	74	73	72	72	71
30	76	75	74	73	73	72
31	78	77	76	75	74	73
32	80	79	78	77	76	75
33	81	80	79	78	77	76
34	82	81	80	79	78	77
35	84	83	82	81	80	79
36	85	84	83	82	81	80
37	87	86	85	84	83	82
38	88	87	86	85	84	83
39	90	89	88	87	86	85
40	91	90	89	88	87	86
41	92	91	90	89	88	87
42	93	92	91	90	89	88
43	95	94	93	92	91	90
44	96	95	94	93	92	91
45	97	96	95	94	93	92
46	99	98	97	96	95	94
47	100	99	98	97	96	95
48	101	100	99	98	97	96
49	102	101	100	99	98	97
50	103	102	101	100	99	98

Raw Score	4-6	4-7	4-8	4-9	4-10	4-11
51	104	103	102	101	100	99
52	105	104	103	102	101	100
53	107	106	105	104	103	102
54	108	107	106	105	104	103
55	109	108	107	106	105	104
56	110	109	108	107	106	105
57	111	110	109	108	107	106
58	112	111	110	109	108	107
59	113	112	111	110	109	108
60	114	113	112	111	110	109
61	116	115	114	113	112	111
62	117	116	115	114	113	112
63	118	117	116	115	114	113
64	119	118	117	116	115	114
65	120	119	118	117	116	115
66	121	120	119	118	117	116
67	122	121	120	119	118	117
68	123	122	121	120	119	118
69	125	124	123	122	121	120
70	126	125	124	123	122	121
71	127	126	125	124	123	122
72	129	128	127	126	125	124
73	130	129	128	127	126	125
74	132	131	130	129	127	126
75	133	132	131	130	128	127
76	135	134	133	131	130	129
77	137	136	135	133	132	131
78	139	138	136	135	134	132
79	140	139	137	136	135	133
80	142	141	139	138	136	135
81	144	143	141	140	138	137
82	>145	145	143	141	140	138
83		>145	145	143	142	140
84			>145	145	144	142
85				>145	>145	144
86						145
87						>145
88						
89						
90						

TABLE D.1—Conversion of Raw Scores to Standard Scores
Ages 5-0–5-11

Raw Score	5-0 5-1	5-2 5-3	5-4 5-5	5-6 5-7	5-8 5-9	5-10 5-11
16	<55					
17	55	<55				
18	56	55	<55			
19	57	56	55	<55	<55	
20	59	58	57	56	55	<55
21	60	59	58	57	56	55
22	61	60	59	58	57	56
23	62	61	60	59	58	57
24	63	62	61	60	59	58
25	64	63	62	61	60	59
26	65	64	63	62	61	60
27	67	66	65	64	63	62
28	68	67	66	65	64	63
29	70	68	67	66	65	64
30	71	69	68	67	66	65
31	72	71	69	68	67	66
32	74	72	70	69	68	67
33	75	73	71	70	69	68
34	76	75	73	71	70	69
35	78	76	74	72	71	70
36	79	77	75	73	72	71
37	80	78	76	74	73	72
38	82	80	78	76	75	74
39	83	81	79	77	76	75
40	84	82	80	78	77	76
41	85	83	81	79	78	77
42	87	85	83	81	80	78
43	88	86	84	82	81	79
44	89	87	85	83	82	80
45	90	88	86	84	83	81
46	92	90	88	86	85	83
47	93	91	89	87	86	84
48	94	92	90	88	87	85
49	95	93	91	89	88	86
50	96	94	92	90	89	87
51	97	95	93	91	90	88
52	98	96	94	92	91	89
53	100	98	96	94	92	90
54	101	99	97	95	94	92
55	102	100	98	96	95	93
56	103	101	99	97	96	94
57	104	102	100	98	97	95
58	105	103	101	99	98	96
59	106	104	102	100	99	97
60	107	105	103	101	100	98
61	109	107	105	103	101	99
62	110	108	106	104	102	100
63	111	109	107	105	103	101
64	112	110	108	106	104	102
65	113	111	109	107	105	103
66	114	112	110	108	106	104
67	115	113	111	109	107	105
68	116	114	112	110	108	106
69	118	116	113	111	109	107
70	119	117	114	112	111	109
71	120	118	115	113	112	110
72	122	120	117	115	113	111
73	123	121	118	116	114	112
74	124	122	119	117	115	113
75	125	123	120	118	116	114
76	127	124	121	119	117	115
77	129	126	123	121	119	117
78	130	127	124	122	120	118
79	131	128	125	123	121	119
80	133	130	127	124	122	120
81	135	132	129	126	124	122
82	136	133	130	127	125	123
83	138	135	132	129	127	125
84	139	136	133	130	128	126
85	141	138	135	132	130	127
86	142	139	136	133	131	128
87	144	141	138	135	132	130
88	>145	143	140	137	134	132
89		145	142	139	136	133
90		>145	144	141	138	135
91			>145	143	140	137
92				145	142	139
93				>145	143	140
94					145	142
95					>145	144
96						>145
97						
98						
99						
100						
101						
102						
103						
104						
105						

TABLE D.1—Conversion of Raw Scores to Standard Scores
Ages 6-0–6-11

Raw Score	6-0 6-1	6-2 6-3	6-4 6-5	6-6 6-7	6-8 6-9	6-10 6-11
21	<55					
22	55	<55				
23	56	55	<55	<55		
24	57	56	55	55	<55	
25	58	57	56	56	55	<55
26	59	58	57	57	56	55
27	61	60	59	58	57	56
28	62	61	60	59	58	57
29	63	62	61	60	59	58
30	64	63	62	61	60	59
31	65	64	63	62	61	60
32	66	65	64	63	62	61
33	67	66	65	64	63	62
34	68	67	66	65	64	63
35	69	68	67	66	65	64
36	70	69	68	67	66	65
37	71	70	69	68	67	66
38	72	71	70	69	68	67
39	73	72	71	70	69	68
40	74	73	72	71	70	69
41	75	74	73	72	71	70
42	77	75	74	72	71	70
43	78	76	75	73	72	71
44	79	77	76	74	73	72
45	80	78	77	75	74	73
46	81	80	78	76	75	74
47	82	81	79	77	76	75
48	83	82	80	78	77	76
49	84	83	81	79	78	77
50	85	84	82	80	79	78
51	86	85	83	81	80	79
52	87	86	84	82	81	80
53	89	87	85	83	82	81
54	90	89	87	85	84	83
55	91	90	88	86	85	83
56	92	91	89	87	86	84
57	93	92	90	88	87	85
58	94	93	91	89	88	86
59	95	94	92	90	89	87
60	96	95	93	91	90	88
61	98	96	94	92	91	89
62	99	97	95	93	92	90
63	100	98	96	94	93	91
64	101	99	97	95	94	92
65	102	100	98	96	95	93
66	103	101	99	97	96	94
67	104	102	100	98	97	95
68	105	103	101	99	98	96
69	106	104	102	100	99	97
70	107	106	104	102	100	99
71	108	107	105	103	102	100
72	110	108	106	104	103	101
73	111	109	107	105	104	102
74	112	110	108	106	105	103
75	113	111	109	107	106	104
76	114	112	110	108	107	105
77	115	113	111	109	108	106
78	116	114	112	110	109	107
79	117	115	113	111	110	108
80	118	116	114	112	111	109
81	119	117	115	113	112	110
82	121	119	117	115	113	111
83	122	120	118	116	114	112
84	123	121	119	117	115	113
85	125	123	120	118	116	114
86	126	124	121	119	117	115
87	127	125	122	120	118	116
88	129	127	124	122	120	118
89	131	128	125	123	121	119
90	132	129	126	124	122	120
91	134	131	128	126	124	122
92	136	133	130	127	125	123
93	137	134	131	128	126	124
94	139	136	133	130	128	126
95	141	138	135	132	130	127
96	142	139	136	133	131	128
97	144	141	138	135	132	130
98	>145	143	140	137	134	132
99		145	142	139	136	133
100		>145	144	141	138	135
101			>145	143	140	137
102				145	142	139
103				>145	144	141
104					>145	143
105						145
106						>145
107						
108						
109						
110						

TABLE D.1—Conversion of Raw Scores to Standard Scores
Ages 7-0–7-11

Raw Score	7-0 / 7-1	7-2 / 7-3	7-4 / 7-5	7-6 / 7-7	7-8 / 7-9	7-10 / 7-11
26	<55					
27	55	<55				
28	56	55	<55	<55		
29	57	56	55	55	<55	
30	58	57	56	56	55	<55
31	59	58	57	57	56	55
32	60	59	58	58	57	56
33	61	60	59	59	58	57
34	62	61	60	60	59	58
35	63	62	61	61	60	59
36	64	63	62	61	60	59
37	65	64	63	62	61	60
38	66	65	64	63	62	61
39	67	66	65	64	63	62
40	68	67	66	65	64	63
41	69	68	67	66	65	64
42	69	68	67	66	65	64
43	70	69	68	67	66	65
44	71	70	69	68	67	66
45	72	71	70	69	68	67
46	73	72	71	70	69	68
47	74	73	72	71	70	69
48	75	74	73	72	71	70
49	76	75	74	73	72	71
50	77	76	75	74	73	72
51	78	77	76	75	74	73
52	79	78	77	76	75	74
53	80	79	78	77	76	75
54	81	80	79	78	77	76
55	82	80	79	78	77	76
56	83	81	80	79	78	77
57	84	82	81	80	79	78
58	85	83	82	81	80	79
59	86	84	83	82	81	80
60	87	85	84	83	82	81
61	88	86	85	84	83	82
62	89	87	86	85	84	83
63	90	88	87	86	85	84
64	91	89	88	86	85	84
65	92	90	89	87	86	85
66	93	91	90	88	87	86
67	94	92	91	89	88	87
68	95	93	92	90	89	88
69	96	94	93	91	90	89
70	97	96	94	92	91	90

Raw Score	7-0 / 7-1	7-2 / 7-3	7-4 / 7-5	7-6 / 7-7	7-8 / 7-9	7-10 / 7-11
71	98	97	95	93	92	91
72	99	98	96	94	93	92
73	100	99	97	95	94	93
74	101	100	98	96	95	94
75	102	101	99	97	96	95
76	103	102	100	98	97	96
77	104	103	101	99	98	97
78	105	104	102	100	99	98
79	106	105	103	101	100	99
80	107	106	104	102	101	100
81	108	107	105	103	102	101
82	110	108	106	104	103	102
83	111	109	107	105	104	103
84	112	110	108	106	105	104
85	113	111	109	107	106	104
86	114	112	110	108	107	105
87	115	113	111	109	108	106
88	116	114	112	110	109	107
89	117	115	113	111	110	108
90	118	116	114	112	111	109
91	119	117	115	113	112	110
92	121	119	117	115	114	112
93	122	120	118	116	115	113
94	123	121	119	117	116	114
95	125	123	120	118	117	115
96	126	124	121	119	118	116
97	127	125	122	120	119	117
98	129	127	124	122	121	119
99	131	128	125	123	122	120
100	132	129	126	124	123	121
101	134	131	128	125	124	122
102	136	133	130	127	125	123
103	137	134	131	128	126	124
104	140	136	133	130	128	126
105	142	138	135	132	130	128
106	144	140	136	133	131	129
107	>145	142	138	135	133	131
108		144	140	137	135	132
109		>145	143	140	137	135
110			145	142	139	136
111			>145	144	141	138
112				>145	144	141
113					145	142
114					>145	144
115						>145

Raw Score	8-0 8-1	8-2 8-3	8-4 8-5	8-6 8-7	8-8 8-9	8-10 8-11
26						
27						
28						
29						
30	<55					
31	55	<55				
32	56	55	<55	<55		
33	57	56	55	55	<55	
34	58	57	56	56	55	<55
35	59	58	57	57	56	55
36	59	58	57	57	56	56
37	60	59	58	58	57	57
38	61	60	59	59	58	57
39	62	61	60	60	59	58
40	63	62	61	61	60	59
41	64	63	62	62	61	60
42	64	63	62	62	61	61
43	65	64	63	63	62	61
44	66	65	64	64	63	62
45	67	66	65	65	64	63
46	67	66	65	65	64	64
47	68	67	66	66	65	64
48	69	68	67	67	66	65
49	70	69	68	68	67	66
50	71	70	69	69	68	67
51	72	71	70	69	68	67
52	73	72	71	70	69	68
53	74	73	72	71	70	69
54	75	74	73	72	71	70
55	75	74	73	73	72	71
56	76	75	74	74	73	72
57	77	76	75	74	73	72
58	78	77	76	75	74	73
59	79	78	77	76	75	74
60	80	79	78	77	76	75
61	81	80	79	78	77	76
62	82	81	80	79	78	77
63	83	82	81	80	79	78
64	83	82	81	80	79	78
65	84	83	82	81	80	79
66	85	84	83	82	81	80
67	86	85	84	83	82	81
68	87	86	85	84	83	82
69	88	87	86	85	84	83
70	89	88	87	86	85	84
71	90	89	88	87	86	85
72	90	89	88	87	86	85
73	91	90	89	88	87	86
74	92	91	90	89	88	87
75	93	92	91	90	89	88
76	94	93	92	91	90	89
77	95	94	93	92	91	90
78	96	95	94	92	91	90
79	97	96	95	93	92	91
80	98	97	96	94	93	92
81	99	98	97	95	94	93
82	100	99	98	96	95	94
83	101	100	99	97	96	95
84	102	101	100	98	97	96
85	103	101	100	99	98	97
86	104	102	101	99	98	97
87	105	103	102	100	99	98
88	106	104	103	101	100	99
89	107	105	104	102	101	100
90	108	106	105	103	102	101
91	109	107	106	104	103	102
92	110	109	107	105	104	103
93	111	110	108	106	105	104
94	112	111	109	107	106	105
95	113	112	110	108	107	106
96	114	113	111	109	108	107
97	116	114	113	111	110	109
98	117	116	114	112	111	110
99	118	117	115	113	112	111
100	119	118	116	114	113	112
101	120	119	117	115	114	113
102	122	120	118	116	115	114
103	123	121	119	117	116	115
104	124	122	120	118	117	116
105	126	124	122	120	119	117
106	127	125	123	121	120	118
107	128	126	124	122	121	119
108	130	128	125	123	122	120
109	132	130	127	125	124	122
110	134	131	128	126	125	123
111	135	132	129	127	126	124
112	138	135	132	129	127	125
113	139	136	133	130	128	126
114	141	138	135	132	130	128
115	143	140	137	134	132	130
116	145	142	139	136	134	132
117	>145	144	141	138	136	133
118		>145	144	141	138	136
119			>145	143	140	137
120				>145	143	140
121					145	142
122					>145	144
123						>145
124						
125						

TABLE D.1—Conversion of Raw Scores to Standard Scores
Ages 9-0–9-11

Raw Score	9-0 9-1	9-2 9-3	9-4 9-5	9-6 9-7	9-8 9-9	9-10 9-11
31						
32						
33						
34	<55					
35	55	<55				
36	55	55	<55	<55		
37	56	56	55	55		
38	57	56	55	55	<55	<55
39	58	57	56	56	55	55
40	59	58	57	57	56	56
41	60	59	58	58	57	57
42	60	60	59	59	58	58
43	61	60	59	59	58	58
44	62	61	60	60	59	59
45	63	62	61	61	60	60
46	63	63	62	62	61	61
47	64	63	62	62	61	61
48	65	64	63	63	62	62
49	66	65	64	64	63	63
50	67	66	65	65	64	64
51	67	66	65	65	64	64
52	68	67	66	66	65	65
53	69	68	67	67	66	66
54	70	69	68	68	67	66
55	70	69	68	68	67	67
56	71	70	69	69	68	68
57	72	71	70	70	69	68
58	73	72	71	71	70	69
59	73	72	71	71	70	70
60	74	73	72	72	71	71
61	75	74	73	73	72	71
62	76	75	74	74	73	72
63	77	76	75	75	74	73
64	77	76	75	75	74	73
65	78	77	76	76	75	74
66	79	78	77	77	76	75
67	80	79	78	78	77	76
68	81	80	79	78	77	76
69	82	81	80	79	78	77
70	83	82	81	80	79	78
71	84	83	82	81	80	79
72	84	83	82	82	81	80
73	85	84	83	82	81	80
74	86	85	84	83	82	81
75	87	86	85	84	83	82
76	88	87	86	85	84	83
77	89	88	87	86	85	84
78	89	88	87	86	85	84
79	90	89	88	87	86	85
80	91	90	89	88	87	86
81	92	91	90	89	88	87
82	93	92	91	90	89	88
83	94	93	92	91	90	89
84	95	94	93	92	91	90
85	96	95	94	93	92	91
86	96	95	94	93	92	91
87	97	96	95	94	93	92
88	98	97	96	95	94	93
89	99	98	97	96	95	94
90	100	99	98	97	96	95
91	101	100	99	98	97	96
92	102	101	100	99	98	97
93	103	102	101	99	98	97
94	104	103	102	100	99	98
95	105	104	103	101	100	99
96	106	105	104	102	101	100
97	107	106	105	103	102	101
98	108	107	106	104	103	102
99	109	108	107	105	104	103
100	110	109	108	106	105	104
101	111	110	109	107	106	105
102	112	111	110	108	107	106
103	113	112	111	109	108	107
104	114	113	112	110	109	108
105	116	114	113	111	110	109
106	117	115	114	112	111	110
107	118	116	115	113	112	111
108	119	117	116	114	113	112
109	120	119	117	115	114	113
110	121	120	118	116	115	114
111	122	121	119	117	116	115
112	124	122	120	118	117	116
113	125	123	121	119	118	117
114	127	125	123	121	120	118
115	128	126	124	122	121	119
116	129	127	125	123	122	120
117	131	129	126	124	123	121
118	133	131	128	126	125	123
119	135	132	129	127	126	124
120	137	134	131	129	128	126
121	139	136	133	130	129	127
122	141	138	135	132	130	128
123	143	140	137	134	132	130
124	145	142	139	136	134	132
125	>145	144	141	138	136	134
126		>145	144	141	138	136
127			>145	144	141	138
128				>145	144	141
129					>145	143
130						>145

TABLE D.1—Conversion of Raw Scores to Standard Scores
Ages 10-0–10-11

Raw Score	10-0 / 10-1	10-2 / 10-3	10-4 / 10-5	10-6 / 10-7	10-8 / 10-9	10-10 / 10-11
36						
37						
38						
39	<55	<55				
40	55	55	<55	<55		
41	56	56	55	55	<55	<55
42	57	57	56	56	55	55
43	57	57	56	56	56	55
44	58	58	57	57	56	56
45	59	59	58	58	57	57
46	60	60	59	59	58	58
47	60	60	59	59	59	58
48	61	61	60	60	59	59
49	62	62	61	61	60	60
50	63	63	62	62	61	61
51	63	63	62	62	62	61
52	64	64	63	63	62	62
53	65	65	64	64	63	63
54	66	65	64	64	63	63
55	66	66	65	65	64	64
56	67	67	66	66	65	65
57	68	67	66	66	65	65
58	69	68	67	67	66	66
59	69	69	68	68	67	67
60	70	70	69	69	68	67
61	71	70	69	69	68	68
62	72	71	70	70	69	69
63	73	72	71	71	70	69
64	73	72	71	71	70	70
65	74	73	72	72	71	71
66	75	74	73	73	72	72
67	75	74	73	73	73	72
68	76	75	74	74	73	73
69	77	76	75	75	74	74
70	78	77	76	76	75	74
71	78	77	76	76	75	75
72	79	78	77	77	76	75
73	80	79	78	78	77	76
74	80	79	78	78	77	77
75	81	80	79	79	78	77
76	82	81	80	80	79	78
77	83	82	81	81	80	79
78	83	82	81	81	80	79
79	84	83	82	82	81	80
80	85	84	83	83	82	81
81	86	85	84	84	83	82
82	87	86	85	84	83	82
83	88	87	86	85	84	83
84	89	88	87	86	85	84
85	90	89	88	87	86	85
86	90	89	88	88	87	86
87	91	90	89	88	87	86
88	92	91	90	89	88	87
89	93	92	91	90	89	88
90	94	93	92	91	90	89
91	95	94	93	92	91	90
92	96	95	94	93	92	91
93	96	95	94	93	92	91
94	97	96	95	94	93	92
95	98	97	96	95	94	93
96	99	98	97	96	95	94
97	100	99	98	97	96	95
98	101	100	99	98	97	96
99	102	101	100	99	98	97
100	103	102	101	100	99	98
101	103	102	101	100	99	98
102	104	103	102	101	100	99
103	105	104	103	102	101	100
104	106	105	104	103	102	101
105	107	106	105	104	103	102
106	108	107	106	105	104	103
107	109	108	107	106	105	104
108	110	109	108	107	106	105
109	111	110	109	108	107	106
110	112	111	110	109	108	107
111	113	112	111	110	109	108
112	114	113	112	111	110	109
113	115	114	113	111	110	109
114	117	115	114	112	111	110
115	118	116	115	113	112	111
116	119	117	116	114	113	112
117	120	118	117	115	114	113
118	122	120	119	117	116	115
119	123	121	120	118	117	116
120	124	123	121	119	118	117
121	125	124	122	120	119	118
122	127	125	123	121	120	119
123	128	126	124	122	121	120
124	130	128	126	124	123	122
125	131	129	127	125	124	123
126	133	131	128	126	125	124
127	136	133	130	128	127	125
128	138	135	132	130	129	127
129	140	137	134	131	130	128
130	143	139	136	133	132	130
131	145	142	138	135	133	131
132	>145	144	141	138	136	134
133		>145	144	141	139	136
134			>145	144	141	138
135				>145	143	140
136					>145	143
137						>145
138						
139						
140						
141						
142						
143						
144						
145						

TABLE D.1—Conversion of Raw Scores to Standard Scores
Ages 11-0–11-11

Raw Score	11-0 11-2	11-3 11-5	11-6 11-8	11-9 11-11
41				
42	<55			
43	55			
44	55	<55	<55	
45	56	55	55	<55
46	57	56	56	55
47	58	57	57	56
48	58	57	57	56
49	59	58	58	57
50	60	59	59	58
51	61	60	60	59
52	61	60	60	59
53	62	61	61	60
54	62	61	61	60
55	63	62	62	61
56	64	63	63	62
57	64	63	63	62
58	65	64	64	63
59	66	65	65	64
60	67	66	65	64
61	67	66	66	65
62	68	67	67	66
63	69	68	67	66
64	69	68	68	67
65	70	69	69	68
66	71	70	70	69
67	72	71	71	70
68	72	71	71	70
69	73	72	72	71
70	74	73	72	71
71	74	73	73	72
72	75	74	73	72
73	76	75	74	73
74	76	75	75	74
75	77	76	75	74
76	78	77	76	75
77	79	78	77	76
78	79	78	77	76
79	80	79	78	77
80	81	80	79	78
81	81	80	79	78
82	82	81	80	79
83	83	82	81	80
84	84	83	82	81
85	84	83	82	81
86	85	84	83	82
87	86	85	84	83
88	87	86	85	84
89	87	86	85	84
90	88	87	86	85
91	89	88	87	86
92	90	89	88	87
93	90	89	88	87
94	91	90	89	88
95	92	91	90	89

Raw Score	11-0 11-2	11-3 11-5	11-6 11-8	11-9 11-11
96	93	92	91	90
97	93	92	91	90
98	94	93	92	91
99	95	94	93	92
100	96	95	93	92
101	97	96	94	93
102	97	96	95	94
103	98	97	96	95
104	99	98	97	96
105	100	99	97	96
106	101	100	98	97
107	102	101	99	98
108	103	102	100	99
109	104	103	101	100
110	105	104	102	101
111	106	105	103	102
112	107	106	104	103
113	108	106	104	103
114	109	107	105	104
115	110	108	106	105
116	111	109	107	106
117	112	110	108	107
118	113	111	109	108
119	114	112	110	109
120	115	113	111	110
121	116	114	112	111
122	117	115	113	112
123	118	116	114	113
124	120	118	116	114
125	121	119	117	115
126	122	120	118	116
127	123	121	119	117
128	125	122	120	119
129	126	124	122	120
130	128	125	123	121
131	129	126	124	122
132	131	128	125	123
133	133	130	127	125
134	135	132	129	127
135	137	133	130	128
136	140	135	132	130
137	142	138	134	131
138	144	140	136	133
139	>145	142	138	135
140		145	140	137
141		>145	143	140
142			>145	143
143				>145
144				
145				
146				
147				
148				
149				
150				

Raw Score	12-0 12-2	12-3 12-5	12-6 12-8	12-9 12-11	Raw Score	12-0 12-2	12-3 12-5	12-6 12-8	12-9 12-11
46	<55				101	92	91	90	89
47	55	<55	<55		102	93	92	91	90
48	56	55	55	<55	103	94	93	92	91
49	57	56	56	55	104	95	94	93	92
50	57	56	56	55	105	95	94	93	92
51	58	57	57	56	106	96	95	94	93
52	59	58	58	57	107	97	96	95	94
53	59	58	58	57	108	98	97	96	95
54	60	59	59	58	109	99	98	96	95
55	61	60	60	59	110	99	98	97	96
56	61	60	60	59	111	100	99	98	97
57	62	61	61	60	112	101	100	99	98
58	63	62	62	61	113	102	101	99	98
59	63	62	62	61	114	103	102	100	99
60	64	63	63	62	115	104	103	101	100
61	65	64	64	63	116	105	104	102	101
62	65	64	64	63	117	106	105	103	102
63	66	65	65	64	118	107	106	104	103
64	67	66	66	65	119	108	107	105	104
65	67	66	66	65	120	109	108	106	105
66	68	67	67	66	121	109	108	106	105
67	69	68	68	67	122	110	109	107	106
68	69	68	68	67	123	111	110	108	107
69	70	69	69	68	124	113	111	109	108
70	70	69	69	68	125	114	112	110	109
71	71	70	70	69	126	115	113	111	110
72	72	71	71	70	127	116	114	112	111
73	72	71	71	70	128	117	116	114	113
74	73	72	72	71	129	119	117	115	114
75	74	73	73	72	130	120	118	116	115
76	74	73	73	72	131	121	119	117	116
77	75	74	74	73	132	122	120	118	117
78	75	74	74	73	133	123	121	119	118
79	76	75	75	74	134	124	122	120	119
80	77	76	76	75	135	125	123	121	120
81	77	76	76	75	136	127	125	123	122
82	78	77	77	76	137	129	126	124	123
83	79	78	78	77	138	130	127	125	124
84	80	79	78	77	139	132	129	126	125
85	80	79	79	78	140	134	131	128	126
86	81	80	80	79	141	136	133	130	128
87	82	81	80	79	142	139	135	132	130
88	83	82	81	80	143	142	137	134	132
89	83	82	82	81	144	144	140	136	133
90	84	83	82	81	145	>145	143	139	136
91	85	84	83	82	146		145	141	138
92	86	85	84	83	147		>145	143	140
93	86	85	84	83	148			>145	143
94	87	86	85	84	149				145
95	88	87	86	85	150				>145
96	89	88	87	86	151				
97	89	88	87	86	152				
98	90	89	88	87	153				
99	91	90	89	88	154				
100	91	90	89	88	155				

TABLE D.1—Conversion of Raw Scores to Standard Scores
Ages 13-0–13-11

Raw Score	13-0 13-2	13-3 13-5	13-6 13-8	13-9 13-11	Raw Score	13-0 13-2	13-3 13-5	13-6 13-8	13-9 13-11
46					101	88	87	86	85
47					102	89	88	87	86
48					103	90	89	88	87
49	<55				104	91	90	89	88
50	55	<55	<55		105	91	90	89	88
51	56	55	55		106	92	91	90	89
52	56	55	55	<55	107	93	92	91	90
53	57	56	56	55	108	94	93	92	91
54	58	57	57	56	109	94	93	92	91
55	58	57	57	56	110	95	94	93	92
56	59	58	58	57	111	96	95	94	93
57	60	59	59	58	112	97	96	95	94
58	60	59	59	58	113	97	96	95	94
59	61	60	60	59	114	98	97	96	95
60	62	61	61	60	115	99	98	97	96
61	62	61	61	60	116	100	99	98	97
62	63	62	62	61	117	101	100	99	98
63	64	63	63	62	118	102	101	100	99
64	64	63	63	62	119	102	101	100	99
65	65	64	64	63	120	103	102	101	100
66	66	65	65	64	121	104	103	102	101
67	66	65	65	64	122	105	104	103	102
68	67	66	66	65	123	106	105	104	103
69	68	67	67	66	124	107	106	105	104
70	68	67	67	66	125	108	107	106	105
71	69	68	68	67	126	109	108	107	106
72	69	68	68	67	127	110	109	108	107
73	70	69	69	68	128	111	110	109	108
74	71	70	70	69	129	112	111	110	109
75	71	70	70	69	130	113	112	111	110
76	72	71	71	70	131	114	113	112	111
77	73	72	72	71	132	115	114	113	112
78	73	72	72	71	133	116	115	114	113
79	74	73	73	72	134	118	117	115	114
80	74	73	73	72	135	119	118	116	115
81	75	74	74	73	136	120	119	117	116
82	76	75	75	74	137	121	120	118	117
83	76	75	75	74	138	122	121	119	118
84	77	76	76	75	139	123	122	120	119
85	77	76	76	75	140	125	123	121	120
86	78	77	77	76	141	126	124	122	121
87	79	78	78	77	142	128	126	124	123
88	79	78	78	77	143	129	127	125	124
89	80	79	79	78	144	131	128	126	125
90	80	79	79	78	145	133	130	128	127
91	81	80	80	79	146	135	132	130	128
92	82	81	81	80	147	137	134	131	129
93	82	81	81	80	148	140	137	134	132
94	83	82	82	81	149	142	139	136	134
95	84	83	83	82	150	145	142	139	136
96	85	84	83	82	151	>145	144	141	138
97	85	84	84	83	152		>145	144	141
98	86	85	84	83	153			>145	142
99	87	86	85	84	154				145
100	87	86	86	85	155				>145

TABLE D.1—Conversion of Raw Scores to Standard Scores
Ages 14-0–15-11

Raw Score	14-0 14-3	14-4 14-7	14-8 14-11	15-0 15-3	15-4 15-7	15-8 15-11
51						
52	<55					
53	55	<55				
54	56	55	<55			
55	56	55	55	<55		
56	57	56	55	55	<55	
57	58	57	56	56	55	<55
58	58	57	57	56	56	55
59	59	58	57	57	56	55
60	60	59	58	58	57	56
61	60	59	59	58	58	57
62	61	60	59	59	58	57
63	62	61	60	60	59	58
64	62	61	61	60	60	59
65	63	62	61	61	60	59
66	63	62	62	61	61	60
67	64	63	63	62	62	61
68	65	64	63	63	62	61
69	65	64	64	63	63	62
70	66	65	65	64	64	63
71	67	66	65	65	64	63
72	67	66	66	65	65	64
73	68	67	66	66	65	64
74	69	68	67	67	66	65
75	69	68	68	67	67	66
76	70	69	68	68	67	66
77	70	69	69	68	68	67
78	71	70	69	69	68	67
79	72	71	70	70	69	68
80	72	71	71	70	70	69
81	73	72	71	71	70	69
82	73	72	72	71	71	70
83	74	73	72	72	71	70
84	75	74	73	73	72	71
85	75	74	74	73	73	72
86	76	75	74	74	73	72
87	76	75	75	74	74	73
88	77	76	75	75	74	73
89	78	77	76	76	75	74
90	78	77	76	76	75	74
91	79	78	77	77	76	75
92	79	78	78	77	77	76
93	80	79	78	78	77	76
94	80	79	79	78	78	77
95	81	80	79	79	78	77
96	81	80	80	79	79	78
97	82	81	80	80	79	78
98	83	82	81	81	80	79
99	83	82	81	81	80	79
100	84	83	82	82	81	80
101	85	84	83	82	81	80
102	85	84	83	83	82	81
103	86	85	84	84	83	82
104	86	85	84	84	83	82
105	87	86	85	85	84	83
106	88	87	86	85	84	83
107	89	88	87	86	85	84
108	89	88	87	87	86	85
109	90	89	88	87	86	85
110	91	90	89	88	87	86

Raw Score	14-0 14-3	14-4 14-7	14-8 14-11	15-0 15-3	15-4 15-7	15-8 15-11
111	91	90	89	89	88	87
112	92	91	90	89	88	87
113	93	92	91	90	89	88
114	94	93	92	91	90	89
115	94	93	92	91	90	89
116	95	94	93	92	91	90
117	96	95	94	93	92	91
118	97	96	95	94	93	92
119	98	97	96	95	94	93
120	99	98	97	96	95	94
121	99	98	97	96	95	94
122	100	99	98	97	96	95
123	101	100	99	98	97	96
124	102	101	100	99	98	97
125	103	102	101	100	99	98
126	104	103	102	101	100	99
127	105	104	103	102	101	100
128	106	105	104	103	102	101
129	107	106	105	103	102	101
130	108	107	106	104	103	102
131	109	108	107	105	104	103
132	110	109	108	106	105	104
133	111	110	109	107	106	105
134	113	111	110	108	107	106
135	114	112	111	109	108	107
136	115	113	112	110	109	108
137	116	114	113	111	110	109
138	117	115	114	112	111	110
139	118	116	115	113	112	111
140	119	117	116	114	113	112
141	120	118	117	115	114	113
142	121	119	118	116	115	114
143	122	120	119	117	116	115
144	123	121	120	118	117	116
145	125	123	121	120	118	117
146	126	124	122	121	119	118
147	127	125	123	122	120	119
148	129	126	124	123	121	120
149	131	128	126	124	123	121
150	133	130	128	126	125	123
151	135	132	129	127	126	124
152	137	133	131	129	127	125
153	139	135	133	131	128	126
154	142	139	136	133	131	128
155	145	141	138	135	132	129
156	>145	144	141	138	135	132
157		>145	144	141	137	134
158			>145	143	139	136
159				>145	143	138
160					>145	140
161						143
162						>145
163						
164						
165						
166						
167						
168						
169						
170						

TABLE D.1—Conversion of Raw Scores to Standard Scores
Ages 16-0–17-11

Raw Score	16-0 16-3	16-4 16-7	16-8 16-11	17-0 17-3	17-4 17-7	17-8 17-11	Raw Score	16-0 16-3	16-4 16-7	16-8 16-11	17-0 17-3	17-4 17-7	17-8 17-11
51							111	87	86	85	85	84	83
52							112	87	86	86	85	85	84
53							113	88	87	86	86	85	84
54							114	89	88	87	87	86	85
55							115	89	88	88	87	87	86
56							116	90	89	88	88	87	86
57	<55						117	91	90	89	89	88	87
58	55						118	92	91	90	90	89	88
59	55	<55	<55				119	93	92	91	90	89	88
60	56	55	55	<55	<55		120	93	92	91	91	90	89
61	57	56	56	55	55		121	94	93	92	92	91	90
62	57	56	56	55	55	<55	122	95	94	93	93	92	91
63	58	57	57	56	56	55	123	96	95	94	93	92	91
64	59	58	58	57	57	56	124	96	95	94	94	93	92
65	59	58	58	58	57	57	125	97	96	95	95	94	93
66	60	59	59	58	58	57	126	98	97	96	96	95	94
67	61	60	60	59	59	58	127	99	98	97	97	96	95
68	61	60	60	59	59	58	128	100	99	98	97	96	95
69	62	61	61	60	60	59	129	100	99	98	98	97	96
70	63	62	62	61	61	60	130	101	100	99	99	98	97
71	63	62	62	61	61	60	131	102	101	100	100	99	98
72	64	63	63	62	62	61	132	103	102	101	101	100	99
73	64	63	63	63	62	62	133	104	103	102	102	101	100
74	65	64	64	63	63	62	134	105	104	103	102	101	100
75	66	65	65	64	64	63	135	106	105	104	103	102	101
76	66	65	65	65	64	64	136	107	106	105	104	103	102
77	67	66	66	65	65	64	137	108	107	106	105	104	103
78	67	66	66	66	65	65	138	109	108	107	106	105	104
79	68	67	67	67	66	66	139	110	109	108	107	106	105
80	69	68	68	67	67	66	140	111	110	109	108	107	106
81	69	68	68	68	67	67	141	112	111	110	109	108	107
82	70	69	69	68	68	67	142	113	112	111	110	109	108
83	70	69	69	69	68	68	143	114	113	112	111	110	109
84	71	70	70	70	69	69	144	115	114	113	112	111	110
85	72	71	71	70	70	69	145	116	115	114	113	112	111
86	72	71	71	71	70	70	146	117	116	115	114	113	112
87	73	72	72	71	71	70	147	118	117	116	115	114	113
88	73	72	72	72	71	71	148	119	118	117	116	115	114
89	74	73	73	73	72	72	149	120	119	118	117	116	115
90	74	73	73	73	72	72	150	122	120	119	118	117	116
91	75	74	74	74	73	73	151	123	121	120	119	118	117
92	76	75	75	74	74	73	152	124	122	121	120	119	118
93	76	75	75	75	74	74	153	125	124	123	122	121	120
94	77	76	76	75	75	74	154	127	125	124	123	122	121
95	77	76	76	76	75	75	155	128	126	125	124	123	122
96	78	77	77	76	76	75	156	129	128	127	126	125	124
97	78	77	77	77	76	76	157	131	130	129	128	127	126
98	79	78	78	77	77	76	158	133	132	131	129	128	127
99	79	78	78	78	77	77	159	135	134	132	131	129	128
100	80	79	79	78	78	77	160	137	136	134	133	131	130
101	80	79	79	79	78	78	161	140	138	136	135	133	131
102	81	80	80	79	79	78	162	143	141	139	137	135	133
103	82	81	81	80	80	79	163	145	144	142	140	138	136
104	82	81	81	80	80	79	164	>145	>145	144	143	141	139
105	83	82	82	81	81	80	165			>145	>145	144	142
106	83	82	82	81	81	80	166					>145	145
107	84	83	83	82	82	81	167						>145
108	85	84	84	83	83	82	168						
109	85	84	84	83	83	82	169						
110	86	85	85	84	84	83	170						

TABLE D.1—Conversion of Raw Scores to Standard Scores
Ages 18-0–18-11

Raw Score	18-0 18-3	18-4 18-7	18-8 18-11		Raw Score	18-0 18-3	18-4 18-7	18-8 18-11
61					116	86	86	85
62	<55				117	87	87	86
63	55	<55			118	88	87	86
64	56	55	<55		119	88	88	87
65	57	56	55		120	89	89	88
66	57	56	55		121	90	89	88
67	58	57	56		122	91	90	89
68	58	58	57		123	91	91	90
69	59	59	58		124	92	91	90
70	60	59	58		125	93	92	91
71	60	60	59		126	94	93	92
72	61	61	60		127	95	94	93
73	62	61	60		128	95	95	94
74	62	62	61		129	96	95	94
75	63	63	62		130	97	96	95
76	64	63	62		131	98	97	96
77	64	64	63		132	99	98	97
78	65	64	63		133	100	99	98
79	66	65	64		134	100	100	99
80	66	66	65		135	101	101	100
81	67	66	65		136	102	102	101
82	67	67	66		137	103	103	102
83	68	67	67		138	104	103	102
84	69	68	67		139	105	104	103
85	69	69	68		140	106	105	104
86	70	69	68		141	107	106	105
87	70	70	69		142	108	107	106
88	71	70	70		143	109	108	107
89	72	71	70		144	110	109	108
90	72	71	71		145	111	110	109
91	73	72	72		146	112	111	110
92	73	73	72		147	113	113	112
93	74	73	73		148	114	114	113
94	74	74	73		149	115	115	114
95	75	74	74		150	116	116	115
96	75	75	74		151	117	117	116
97	76	75	75		152	118	118	117
98	76	76	75		153	120	119	118
99	77	76	76		154	121	120	119
100	77	77	76		155	122	122	121
101	78	77	77		156	123	123	122
102	78	78	77		157	125	124	123
103	79	79	78		158	126	125	124
104	79	79	78		159	127	127	126
105	80	80	79		160	129	128	127
106	80	80	79		161	130	129	128
107	81	81	80		162	132	131	130
108	82	81	80		163	135	134	133
109	82	82	81		164	138	137	136
110	83	82	81		165	141	140	139
111	83	83	82		166	145	144	143
112	84	84	83		167	>145	>145	>145
113	84	84	83		168			
114	85	85	84		169			
115	86	85	84		170			

TABLE D.2
Conversion of Standard Scores to Percentile Ranks and Other Commonly Used Scores

Standard Scores	Percentile Ranks	NCEs	T-Scores	Scaled Scores	Stanines	Standard Scores	Percentile Ranks	NCEs	T-Scores	Scaled Scores	Stanines
< 55	<1	1	<20	1	1	105	63	57	53	11	6
56	<1	1	20	1	1	106	66	58	54	11	6
57	<1	1	21	1	1	107	68	60	55	11	6
58	<1	1	21	2	1	108	70	61	55	12	6
59	<1	1	22	2	1	109	73	63	56	12	6
60	<1	1	23	2	1	110	75	64	57	12	6
61	<1	1	23	2	1	111	77	65	57	12	6
62	1	1	24	2	1	112	79	67	58	12	7
63	1	1	25	3	1	113	81	68	59	13	7
64	1	1	26	3	1	114	83	70	59	13	7
65	1	1	27	3	1	115	84	71	60	13	7
66	1	2	27	3	1	116	86	72	61	13	7
67	1	4	28	3	1	117	87	74	61	13	7
68	2	5	29	4	1	118	88	75	62	14	8
69	2	6	29	4	1	119	90	77	63	14	8
70	2	8	30	4	1	120	91	78	63	14	8
71	3	9	31	4	1	121	92	79	64	14	8
72	3	11	31	4	1	122	93	81	65	14	8
73	4	12	32	5	2	123	94	82	65	15	8
74	4	13	33	5	2	124	95	84	66	15	8
75	5	15	33	5	2	125	95	85	67	15	8
76	5	16	34	5	2	126	96	87	67	15	9
77	6	18	35	5	2	127	96	88	68	15	9
78	7	19	35	6	2	128	97	89	69	16	9
79	8	21	36	6	2	129	97	91	69	16	9
80	9	22	37	6	2	130	98	92	70	16	9
81	10	23	37	6	2	131	98	94	71	16	9
82	11	25	38	6	3	132	98	95	71	16	9
83	13	26	39	7	3	133	99	96	72	17	9
84	14	28	39	7	3	134	99	98	73	17	9
85	16	29	40	7	3	135	99	99	73	17	9
86	18	30	41	7	3	136	99	99	74	17	9
87	19	32	41	7	3	137	99	99	75	17	9
88	21	33	42	8	3	138	99	99	75	18	9
89	23	35	43	8	4	139	>99	99	76	18	9
90	25	36	43	8	4	140	>99	99	77	18	9
91	27	37	44	8	4	141	>99	99	77	18	9
92	30	39	45	8	4	142	>99	99	78	18	9
93	32	40	45	9	4	143	>99	99	79	19	9
94	34	42	46	9	4	144	>99	99	79	19	9
95	37	43	47	9	4	145	>99	99	80	19	9
96	39	44	47	9	5	> 145	> 99	99	>80	19	9
97	42	46	48	9	5						
98	45	47	49	10	5						
99	47	49	49	10	5						
100	50	50	50	10	5						
101	53	51	51	10	5						
102	55	53	51	10	5						
103	58	54	52	11	5						
104	61	56	53	11	6						

TABLE D.3
Conversion of Raw Scores to Age Equivalents

Raw Score	Age Equivalent	Raw Score	Age Equivalent	Raw Score	Age Equivalent
1	1-0	51	4-10	101	10-6
2	1-1	52	4-11	102	10-8
3	1-1	53	5-0	103	10-10
4	1-2	54	5-1	104	11-0
5	1-2	55	5-2	105	11-2
6	1-3	56	5-3	106	11-4
7	1-3	57	5-5	107	11-5
8	1-4	58	5-6	108	11-7
9	1-5	59	5-7	109	11-9
10	1-5	60	5-8	110	11-11
11	1-6	61	5-9	111	12-1
12	1-7	62	5-10	112	12-3
13	1-7	63	6-0	113	12-5
14	1-8	64	6-1	114	12-7
15	1-9	65	6-2	115	12-10
16	1-10	66	6-3	116	12-11
17	1-11	67	6-5	117	13-1
18	2-0	68	6-6	118	13-4
19	2-1	69	6-7	119	13-6
20	2-2	70	6-8	120	13-9
21	2-3	71	6-10	121	13-11
22	2-3	72	6-11	122	14-2
23	2-4	73	7-0	123	14-5
24	2-5	74	7-1	124	14-9
25	2-6	75	7-3	125	15-0
26	2-7	76	7-4	126	15-3
27	2-8	77	7-5	127	15-6
28	2-9	78	7-7	128	15-9
29	2-10	79	7-8	129	16-1
30	2-11	80	7-10	130	16-6
31	3-0	81	7-11	131	16-11
32	3-1	82	8-0	132	17-3
33	3-2	83	8-2	133	17-8
34	3-3	84	8-3	134	18-2
35	3-4	85	8-5	135	18-10
36	3-5	86	8-6	136–170	>19
37	3-6	87	8-7		
38	3-7	88	8-9		
39	3-8	89	8-11		
40	3-10	90	9-0		
41	3-11	91	9-2		
42	4-0	92	9-3		
43	4-1	93	9-5		
44	4-2	94	9-6		
45	4-3	95	9-8		
46	4-4	96	9-10		
47	4-5	97	10-0		
48	4-6	98	10-1		
49	4-8	99	10-3		
50	4-9	100	10-5		

Note: Age equivalents below 2-6 and above 18-5 are extrapolated.

TABLE D.4
Standard Score Differences Between the EOWPVT and ROWPVT
Needed for Statistical Significance

Age Group	Significance Level			
	.15	.10	.05	.01
2	7–8	9	10–12	13+
3	6	7	8–10	11+
4	6	7	8–10	11+
5	6	7–8	9–11	12+
6	6	7	8–10	11+
7	6	7–8	9–11	12+
8	7	8	9–11	12+
9	5	6	7–8	9+
10	6	7	8–10	11+
11	6	7	8–9	10+
12	5	6	7–8	9+
13	4	5	6–7	8+
14	4	5	6–7	8+
15–16	5	6	7–8	9+
17–18	5	6	7–8	9+
Median	6	7	8–10	11+

TABLE D.5
EOWPVT–ROWPVT Standard Score Differences
Obtained by the Standardization Sample

Age Group	Frequency in Standardization Sample						
	>25%	25%	20%	15%	10%	5%	1%
2	0–13	14	15–16	17–20	21–23	24–31	32+
3	0–14	15–16	17	18–22	23–25	26–31	32+
4	0–13	14	15–16	17	18–21	22–27	28+
5	0–12	13–14	15	16–18	19–23	24–29	30+
6	0–12	13	14–15	16–19	20–22	23–30	31+
7	0–12	13	14	15–18	19–21	22–28	29+
8	0–11	12–14	15–16	17–18	19–20	21–29	30+
9	0–11	12–13	14–15	16–17	18–22	23–28	29+
10	0–10	11	12–13	14–16	17–20	21–26	27+
11	0–9	10–11	12	13–14	15–16	17–18	19+
12	0–10	11–12	13–14	15–16	17	18–21	22+
13	0–10	11	12–13	14–15	16–18	19–24	25+
14	0–8	9–10	11	12–14	15–19	20–24	25+
15–16	0–10	11	12	13–14	15–19	20–30	31+
17–18	0–9	10	11–12	14	15–17	18–29	30+
Median	0–11	12–13	14	15–17	18-20	21–28	29+